# CYBERSECURITY FOR BEGINNERS

Learn how to defend yourself from cyberattacks and strengthen your online position by becoming an expert in digital defense.

## DMITRI WILLIAMS

Copyright © Under international copyright law, all rights reserved. This book is a legal treasure. Without the prior written consent of the copyright owner, no part of the contents or cover may be produced in any form or by any means, including electronic, mechanical recording, photocopying, or otherwise.

Copyright © 2024  DMITRI WILLIAMS

# Acknowledgement

I sincerely thank everyone who helped to make this cybersecurity for beginners book a reality. We would especially like to thank [Tracy wealth] for all of her help, advice, and insights along our adventure. I would also like to thank my friends, family, and coworkers for their support and tolerance while I was writing. Finally, I would like to express my gratitude to the readers of this book, whose inquisitiveness and desire to learn have motivated me to undertake this project. Thank you all for making it happen.

**Table of contents**

Introduction to Cybersecurity

Chapter 1

1.1  Understanding Cyber Threats

1.2  Types of Cyber Threats

1.3  Attack Vectors

1.4  The Motivations Behind Cyber Threats

1.5  Impact of Cyber Threats

1.6  Importance of Cybersecurity Awareness

1.7  Basics of Computing and Networking

## 1.8 Interplay Between Computing and Networking

## 1.9 Overview of Computer Systems

### Hardware Components

### Software Components

### Types of Computers

### Computer Architecture

### Networking and Communication

### Security and Privacy

**1.10 Introduction to Networks and the Internet**

**Chapter 2**

**2.1 Fundamentals of Cyber Attacks**

**2.2 Definition of Cyber Attacks**

**2.3 Importance of understanding cyber attacks**

**2.4 Types of Cyber Attacks**

**2.5 Cybersecurity measures**

**2.6 Techniques used in cyber attacks**

**2.7 Cybersecurity Tools and Technologies**

2.8 Encryption Basics

Chapter 3

3.1 Securing Personal Devices in cybersecurity

3.2 How to secure your home WiFi network

3.3 How to protect yourself from phishing attacks

3.4 Signs of a phishing email

3.5 Firewalls in cybersecurity

3.6 Protecting Your Computer

### 3.7 Safe Browsing Practices

### Chapter 4

### 4.1 Securing Internet of Things (IoT) Devices

### 4.2 Introduction to Cyber Hygiene

### 4.3 Benefits of Cyber Hygiene

### 4.4 Common Cyber Hygiene Problems

### 4.5 Regular Software Updates

### 4.6 Data Backup Practices

### Chapter 5

## 5.1 Cybersecurity Best Practices for Businesses

## 5.2 Employee Training and Awareness

## 5.3 Incident Response and Recovery

## 5.4 Steps to take after a security breach

## 5.5 Data Recovery Techniques

# Chapter 6

## 6.1 Emerging Trends in Cybersecurity

## 6.2 How to implement Zero Trust in your organization

## 6.3 How to handle legacy systems within a Zero Trust framework

## 6.4 Common features of endpoint security solutions

## 6.5 Supply Chain Security

## 6.6 How to assess the security posture of your supply chain partners

## 6.7 Cybersecurity Skills Gap

## 6.8 Artificial Intelligence and Machine Learning in Security

## 6.9 Blockchain Technology for Enhanced Security

6.10 Ethical Considerations in Cybersecurity

6.11 Ethical Hacking and Penetration Testing

Chapter 7

7.1　Careers in Cybersecurity

7.2　Overview of Cybersecurity Roles

7.3　Education and Certification Paths

7.4　Conclusion

7.5 Appendix

# Introduction to Cybersecurity

In our world today, there is no way to overestimate the importance of cybersecurity in our technology driven world. Thus, safeguarding networks, systems, and data from online threats is known as cybersecurity. Attackers may target people, companies, or even whole countries with these planned attacks, which could take many different forms such as ransomware, phishing, malware, and social engineering.

To be able to Preserve the confidentiality, availability, and integrity of data is the fundamental purpose of cybersecurity. The three pillars of data security are availability, integrity, and confidentiality. Availability guarantees that systems and data are available when needed, while integrity ensures that data is correct and reliable. An intricate strategy involving technological advancements, rules, regulations, and user education is needed to accomplish these goals.

The term defense in depth, which means putting in place several levels of security measures to guard against different threats, is one of the core concepts of cybersecurity. Access restrictions, intrusion detection systems, firewalls, antivirus programs, and encryption are a few examples of these levels. Organizations are able to establish a strong security posture that is resistant to advanced cyberattacks by implementing a variety of defensive measures.

Everyone who uses technology has at one time or the other been affected positively or negatively by cybersecurity. It's not simply a problem for big businesses or governmental organizations. Everyone should be conscious of using strong, one-of-a-kind passwords, everyone should always exercise caution when sharing sensitive information online, whether it's public or private information and make sure their software and devices are up to date with security patches in order to safeguard their personal information. To safeguard data, intellectual property, and reputation of their clients, businesses must invest in cybersecurity solutions.

In this digital age, and with our increasing reliance on technology. The threat landscape is expanding in concurrence. Cybercriminals are always bringing in new innovations in the way they operate, taking advantage of weaknesses, and creating new strategies to get around security controls. Due to the constantly changing nature of cyber threats, businesses /organizations/individuals must take a proactive approach to cybersecurity, by continuously evaluating the risks, modifying their defenses, and keeping up with new developments.

If we desire to safeguard our financial resources, privacy, and national security, cybersecurity must be treated with all seriousness that it deserves because it is a vital part of our digital civilization. Through proper assimilation and understanding of cybersecurity concepts and the implementation of strong security measures, individuals and businesses may effectively manage risks and guarantee the confidentiality and integrity of their digital assets.

# Chapter 1

## 1.1 Understanding Cyber Threats

It is very important to understand the different kinds of malicious behaviors and digital vulnerabilities that exist in the internet space, as well as the possible effects that these threats may have on people, companies, and society at large. This is known as understanding cyber threats.

## 1.2 Types of Cyber Threats

**Malware:** This is a malicious software that aims to interfere with, harm, or access computer systems without authorization. For instance, trojan horses, worms, viruses, ransomware, and malware are a few examples.

**Phishing:** This can be described as false attempts to obtain private information by posing as a reliable company over the phone, over text, or through emails, including passwords, credit card numbers, and personal information.

**Attacks known as denial of service (DoS):** If for instance, a system or network is overloaded with traffic, it prevents users from making use of it. Also, it disrupts business activities, and might even result in loss of money.

**Social engineering:** This is the psychological manipulation of others to coerce them into disclosing private information or making them to accept activities that jeopardize security.

**Insider threats:** This is a malicious act carried out by workers or contractors who work for a company and use their access rights to commit crimes against the organization or for personal benefit.

**Advanced Persistent Threats (APTs):** This is a highly coordinated cyberattack mostly by nation-state actors or other highly adept criminal gangs that target a particular individual or organization.

## 1.3 Attack Vectors

**Vulnerabilities:** This can be described as vulnerabilities or faults in hardware, software, or network setups that hackers use in obtaining illegal advantage or access to carry out destructive activities.

**Exploits:** This is a strategy or tactic used in exploiting weaknesses in applications or systems. Attackers may buy or create exploits.

**Backdoors:** This is an unapproved access point that developers or attackers have left in software or systems, giving them the ability to get around standard authentication procedures.

## 1.4 The Motivations Behind Cyber Threats

**1. Financial Gain:** Financial gain is a driving force behind a lot of cyberthreats, which include ransomware attacks, identity theft, and the sale of stolen data on the dark web.

**2. Cyber espionage:** This is a tactic used by nation-states and intelligence services to get data that is confidential,they use it to track down enemies, or thwart adversary activities.

**3. Hacktivism:** This is the term for people or organizations with political or ideological goals using cyberattacks to further their views, express disapproval of perceived injustices, or bring attention to social issues.

**4. Cyber Warfare:** This is used for disruption of enemy infrastructure, gathering intelligence, or ruining vital systems, governments and military groups employ cyberattacks as a component of their strategic military operations.

## 1.5 Impact of Cyber Threats

**1.Monetary Losses**: When there are data breaches, system outages, ransom payments, and legal costs that are related to cyberattacks, this can cause businesses to suffer huge financial losses and in most cases the firm or organization that is affected might be forced to close or stop operations making a lot of people to lose their means of livelihood.

**2. Damage to Reputation:** Cyber incidents could damage the reputation of the organization and of course customers' trust might be lost in the process and this could lower their market share, investor confidence, and brand value.

**3. Infractions of privacy:** Identity theft, fraud, and other crimes against privacy are brought about by data breaches that expose people's personal information.

**4. Risks to national security:** If cyberattacks are targeted to the military systems, government institutions, or vital infrastructures, this could make public safety for the general populace to be jeopardized, and it could affect the geopolitical stability, and national security.

In order to effectively respond to cyberattacks, one must be aware of the always changing environment of cybersecurity risks, take proactive steps to reduce vulnerabilities, and implement efficient incident response procedures. To secure digital assets and defend against new threats, individuals, corporations, governments, and cybersecurity experts must work together to make it happen for a safer Internet space.

## 1.6 Importance of Cybersecurity Awareness

In this digital era, having cybersecurity knowledge is very important and cannot be overemphasized because of the rise in frequency and sophistication of cyberattacks that target people, companies, and governments.

**Here are some of the importance of cybersecurity awareness:**

**1. Safeguarding Private and Sensitive Data:** A lot of people on a continuous basis, matter of fact, some on a daily basis exchange their private and sensitive data online more and more. And as a result of the growth of online activities like banking, socializing, and shopping, people that are aware of cybersecurity are better able to protect their data, which includes passwords, bank account information, and personally identifiable information, in order to thwart identity theft, fraud, and privacy violations.

**2. Cyber Attack Prevention:** Most cyberattacks,if not all, like phishing schemes, malware infections, and social engineering techniques, all make use of human flaws instead of technological ones. This cybersecurity awareness enables users to safeguard their devices and themselves from online risks by teaching them about typical attack methods and how to spot and steer clear of activities that are questionable.

**3. Securing Digital Assets:** For you to be able to store, handle, and transport sensitive data and intellectual property, businesses and organizations must rely on digital technologies. Because human mistake or carelessness which most times could be inevitable can unintentionally expose firms to cyber risks like data breaches, financial losses, and reputational harm, thus having cybersecurity knowledge among employees is so important to ensure the confidentiality, integrity, and availability of corporate assets.

**4. Encourages People to Adopt Responsible Online Behavior**: People who are aware of cybersecurity issues are more likely to use strong passwords, establish multi-factor authentication, update software and operating systems on a regular basis, and refrain from risky online activities like downloading unknown attachments or clicking on dubious links. To achieve a safer and more secure digital environment for oneself and others individuals must cultivate the culture of cybersecurity awareness.

**5. Complying with Regulations and Standards:** If you wish to safeguard confidential data, reduce risks, and stay out of trouble with the law and authorities, many of the sectors and organizations are required to adhere to cybersecurity standards and regulations. Organizations can ensure compliance and accountability at all levels by educating their staff about industry best practices, regulatory requirements, and internal data protection, privacy, and security policies through cybersecurity awareness programs.

**6. Building a Cybersecurity Mindset:** Being aware of cybersecurity involves more than just learning new information; it also includes developing a mindset that is watchful, skeptical, and resilient to changing cyberthreats. Individuals and organizations can proactively adjust their security measures and incident response strategies to keep ahead of cyber attackers and limit the impact of cyberattacks by being updated about emerging trends, threat actors' methods, and cybersecurity news and events.

## 1.7 Basics of Computing and Networking

Our modern digital world is based on two essential concepts, they are: computing and networking. Let's discuss in detail about this:

**Computing:** This refers to the practice of using computer technology to carry out particular tasks that have a clear objective. It covers a broad range of applications, including the design and development of hardware and software systems.

**1.Hardware:** This consists of the central processing unit (CPU), RAM, hard drives, SSDs, input/output devices (keyboard, mouse, monitor), peripherals (printers, scanners), and other physical parts of a computer system.

**2. Software:** These are applications and guidelines that provide computers the ability to carry out operations and handle data. This covers system utilities (disk management tools, antivirus software), application software (Microsoft Office, web browsers, games), and operating systems (Windows, macOS, Linux).

**3. Data:** These are information that is processed and stored by computers in a variety of forms, including databases, text, photos, and videos. Software programs have the ability to manipulate, analyze, and alter data to yield results that are meaningful.

**4. Algorithms**: This is a comprehensive guideline or technique which aids in doing calculations or resolving specific problems. The fundamental building blocks of computer programming and software development are algorithms, which controls how data is handled and actions are performed.

**Networking**

In the field of technology, networking refers to the communication and sharing of resources between computers and other electronic devices. The following are some salient points:

**Definition**: A computer network is made up of two or more computers connected by wireless (like Wi-Fi) or wired connections. Data and information are transmitted, exchanged, or shared.

**Setting up a network:** Protocols for communication govern the rules and procedures that govern the transfer of data between devices that are connected. Examples of common protocols are FTP (File Transfer Protocol), HTTP (Hypertext Transfer Protocol), SMTP (Simple Mail Transfer Protocol), and TCP/IP (Transmission Control Protocol/Internet Protocol).

**File Transfer Protocol (FTP):** On a computer network, files can be transferred between a client and a server using the File Transfer Protocol (FTP), on TCP/IP networks, it usually functions. FTP gives users the ability to upload, download, and work with files on a distant server. It is mostly used for file sharing, software upgrades, and website upkeep, among other things.

**Hypertext Transfer Protocol (HTTP):** Applications for collaborative, networked, hypermedia information systems use the Hypertext Transfer Protocol (HTTP). For the World Wide Web, it serves as the cornerstone of data transfer. Regarding the client-server computer model, HTTP is a request-response protocol. Upon requesting a resource from a web server, an HTTP request message is sent by the web browser, acting as the client. If the request is not able to be fulfilled, the server replies with an HTTP response message that contains the resource that was requested. Due of HTTP's statelessness, data about prior requests is not preserved between transactions.

**Simple Mail Transfer Protocol (SMTP) protocol:** An email message can be sent between servers using the Simple Mail Transfer Protocol (SMTP) protocol. In order to retrieve messages from a server, email clients need other protocols like POP3 (Post Office Protocol version 3) and IMAP (Internet Message Access Protocol). These protocols function together with it. SMTP specifies the format, encryption, and mail server-to-mail server relaying of email messages. Because it makes message delivery across the internet possible, it is an essential part of the email ecosystem.

**Transmission Control Protocol/Internet Protocol (TCP/IP):** A collection of communication protocols called Transmission Control Protocol/Internet Protocol (TCP/IP) is used to connect devices over the internet. End-to-end data communication via TCP/IP defines the packetization, addressing, transmission, routing, and reception of data. There are two primary protocols that comprise it:

**Transmission Control Protocol (TCP):** TCP makes sure that data packets traveling over the internet arrive at their destination in a timely manner and in the right order. It controls flow control, fault detection, and the creation and breaking of connections between devices.

**Internet Protocol (IP):** Data packet addressing and routing between devices on a network is handled by IP. It decides how packets are routed from the source to the destination across linked networks and gives each device a unique IP address.

**Devices:** are the hardware components that connect computers and other devices in a network, including hubs, modems, routers, switches, network interface cards (NICs), and cables (fiber optic, Ethernet).

**Network topology:** This refers to the physical or logical arrangement of links and devices. The star, bus, ring, mesh, and hybrid topologies are frequently used in network architecture. Data sharing and communication are made possible by the Internet, a global network of interconnected computer networks that uses the TCP/IP protocol suite. The internet offers access to a multitude of resources, services, and information via email, file sharing, websites, and other online platforms.

**Security:** When we talk about security, we're talking about the policies and processes implemented to protect network infrastructure, data, and communications from unauthorized access, interception, manipulation, and other security threats. Intrusion detection systems (IDS), firewalls, virtual private networks (VPNs), and access control methods are included in this.

## 1.8 Interplay Between Computing and Networking:

The interplay between computing and networking is a very fascinating area that impacts various aspects of technology. Let us have a discourse on some key points:

**1.Client-Server Model:** This is a networking design in which computers, or clients, use a particular network to request and receive resources or services from centralized servers. Emails, file sharing, online browsing, and many other network-based apps make use of the client server model.

**2. Cloud Computing:** This is an approach to computing whereby distant data centers (the cloud) provide services and resources (such as processing power, storage, and apps) that are accessed online. Network infrastructure plays a major role in cloud computing, providing users and businesses with on-demand computing resources.

**3. Distributed Computing:** This could be described as a computing paradigm where several linked computers or devices can share tasks or processing, this is made possible by networking technologies. When it comes to large-scale computational processes and applications, distributed computing offers scalability, fault tolerance, and parallel processing.

### 1.9 Overview of Computer Systems

A computer system consists of a group of devices, software, and hardware that cooperate to carry out different tasks. These components are explained thus:

## Hardware Components

The motherboard, which connects all the hardware components, is one of the physical components of the computer system. Other physical components include the CPU, RAM, storage devices (hard disk drives, solid-state drives), input devices (keyboards, mice), output devices (monitors, printers), and storage devices (RAM).

- **Central Processing Unit (CPU):** This is the brain of the computer that enhances the execution of instructions.

- **Memory (RAM):** This is a temporary storage for data and instructions which will in turn be processed by the CPU.

- **Storage Devices:** Examples include hard disk drives (HDDs), solid-state drives (SSDs), and flash drives to help store data in the long term.

- **Input Devices:** These include keyboards, mice, scanners, etc., used for inputting data and commands.

- **Output Devices:** These are monitors, printers, speakers, etc., used for display and output of processed data.

- **Motherboard:** This is the main circuit board connecting all of the hardware components.

## Software Components

These are instructions and programs that provide the computer system the ability to carry out particular functions. This comprises the operating system (such as Windows, macOS, or Linux), application software (such as word processors, web browsers, and games), utility software (such as disk cleanup tools and antivirus software), and device drivers, which let the operating system talk to hardware.

- **Operating System (OS):** This is what helps to manage hardware resources and provide user interface for interaction.

- **Application Software:** These can be described as programs that are designed for specific/particular tasks, such as word processing, graphic design, or gaming.

- **Utility Software:** This is tools for system maintenance, security, and optimization.

- **Device Drivers:** This is a software that allows the OS to communicate with hardware devices.

## Types of Computers

Let us talk about the fascinating world of computers and the diverse types that it has. Computers come in various shapes, sizes, and capabilities. These are some of the most notable ones:

**I.Supercomputer:** I like to call it the computer machine. These machines are the speed demons of the computing industry. They can handle billions of instructions or data in a second thanks to their thousands of interconnected processors. Applications for supercomputers can be found in nuclear energy research, weather forecasting, and scientific simulations. This was created in 1976 by Roger Cray and is also used in the management of virtual currencies like Bitcoin.

**II. Mainframe Computer:** The capacity of mainframes to accommodate hundreds or thousands of users at once is one of its best hallmarks. They are quite good at running many programs at once. They are perfect for big businesses and make it easy in handling enormous amounts of data, including the telecom and financial industries. Mainframes have a large capacity for storage, excellent performance, and a long lifespan.

**III. Minicomputer:** with this device up to 200 people can be served simultaneously by these medium-sized multiprocessing PCs. It is mostly used in organizations and divisions for accounting, inventory control, and billing duties. Minicomputers help to balance power and size, much like microcontrollers do.

**IV. Workstation Computer:** Workstations are powerful machines mainly used for graphics design, engineering, and scientific simulations. They offer high performance and specialized software tools.

**V. Personal Computer (PC):** This is more of a computer intended for personal use. They come in two primary forms:

- **Desktop Computers:** This kind of computer can be placed at the top of your desk and it offers versatility.
- **Laptops:** This is very Portable and compact, it can be carried around easily to anywhere, it is perfect for on-the-go computing.

**VI. Server Computer:** Servers help other computers or devices to be operational and also helps its ability to function properly. They handle tasks like file storage, web hosting, and manage databases.

**VII. Analog Computer:** These devices help to continually process data using physical quantities (such as voltage or current). Analog computers were prevalent before the digital computers became mainstream.

**VIII. Digital Computer:** This is the most common type mostly used by everyone today, digital computers process data using discrete values (0s and 1s). Ranging from personal computers to servers.

**IX. Hybrid Computer:** This type of computer combines analog and digital components all at once. Hybrid computers offer the best of both worlds. It is mostly used in scientific and industrial applications.

**X. Tablets and Smartphones:** This type comes with a touchscreen, tablets are portable, flat computers. The little computers that we carry around in our pockets are called smartphones. This little device does the work that computers do.

## Computer Architecture

**I. Von Neumann Architecture:** This is a traditional architecture that consists of a CPU, memory, input/output, and a bus system which enables data transfer.

**II. Harvard Architecture:** This helps to separate instruction and data memory, and it allows simultaneous access to both.

**III. Parallel Computing:** It makes use of multiple processors or centers to perform computations seamlessly/simultaneously, and with this it increases the processing speed.

**IV. Distributed Computing:** This enables the spreading of tasks across two or more interconnected computers to achieve a common goal.

### Networking and Communication

**I. Local Area Network (LAN):** This helps to connect your computers or devices no matter the one you're using within a limited geographical area, such as a home, office, or even campus.

**II. Wide Area Network (WAN):** This helps in Connecting computers and devices over a bigger/larger geographical area, typically making use of the internet.

**III. Wireless Communication:** This makes use of radio waves or infrared signals to transmit data without any physical connections whatsoever.

**Security and Privacy**

**I.Firewalls:** These can be described as software or hardware devices that monitor and control incoming and outgoing network traffic. This helps to protect against unauthorized access.

**II. Encryption:** This helps in the Conversion of data into a secure format so as to prevent unauthorized access during transmission or storage.

**III. Antivirus Software:** This helps in detecting and removal of malicious software (malware) from your computers to enable it safeguarded against security threats.

**IV. Authentication:** This helps to properly verify the identity of users or maybe devices accessing a computer system, either through passwords, biometrics, or security tokens.

## 1.10 Introduction to Networks and the Internet

**Brief history**

The first successful link between the University of California, Los Angeles and the Stanford Research Institute was established on October

29, 1969, by the ARPANET (Advanced Research Projects Agency Network), which was later renamed the Internet. Later in the 1960s, of course libraries started networking and automating catalogs outside of ARPANET. Internet technology advanced with the creation of TCP/IP (Transmission Control Protocol and Internet Protocol) in the 1970s, which was a major turning point in the internet even up till today.

Networks and the Internet play a very important role in connecting people, devices, and information globally.

**Networks:** Networks are systems of linked computers and other devices that help to facilitate resource sharing and communication.

Their coverage of different regions can be used to categorize them.

**Internet:** The Internet is a vast global network of networks, with millions of devices connected globally. It facilitates easy communication, information sharing, and access to resources through various services. It relies heavily on the Internet Protocol (IP) and the Transport Control Protocol (TCP) for consistent and reliable data transmission. When we talk about the internet there has to be a little discourse on the world wide web (www).

**World Wide Web (WWW):** This is a collection of interconnected web pages, websites which are accessible by web browsers.

**Email:** Electronic mail enables users to send and receive messages instantly across the Internet space.

# Chapter 2

## 2.1 Fundamentals of Cyber Attacks

Since there is no one, widely-accepted definition of what an attack is in the discourse of cyber security, the process of recognizing an attack is not as simple as it might seem. For instance, is it an attack if the attacker is trying to take advantage of a system's previously undiscovered vulnerability and causes a software crash. Would this be termed as an unintentional denial of service? Should we now conclude that there is a systematic attempt to disrupt the service if the system owner sees recurrent crashes over an extended period of time but is unable to find any evidence of the attacker's presence? It is so important to keep in mind the basic goals and tenets of cyberattacks while also checking the circumstances surrounding a particular incident since these are the kinds of situations that make it challenging to distinguish between unintentional acts and system malfunctions. The importance of information systems to our Internet space is growing massively, and with this growth, so is the scope of cyberattacks, both in terms of frequency and damaging potential. It is now so important to have a solid grasp of what constitutes a cyberattack, the dangers associated with it, and how to create efficient defenses.

## 2.2 Definition of Cyber Attacks

The term "cyber attack" refers to an offensive tactic that uses several techniques to steal, change, or destroy data or information from computer information systems, infrastructures, networks, or personal computers. A sophisticated, well-planned attack on the country's vital infrastructure can be as simple as placing spyware on a computer to steal users' personal data as well as more advanced forms of cyberattack. If one gathers electronically stored information for a social, political, or commercial advantage, this is also another use for cyberattacks. Cyber warfare additionally refers to the employment of cyberattacks to undermine the opposing side in a fight. This could be done in order to assign blame for the attack to a different group or to divulge confidential information that would be harmful to one party. A cyberattack targets cyberspace because its aim is to hinder a person's, group's, or nation's capacity to gain from online use. These attacks have the potential to cause major issues and destroy a great deal of important data. This is extremely concerning since it has the potential to seriously harm a nation's infrastructure and have a big impact on its economy. A cyberattack's ability to inflict damage has continued to increase.

There have been increasing reports that cyberattacks started in the early 1970s and have continued to expand since then. These attacks typically have a motive that is strikingly similar to offline crimes committed in the actual world. The aforementioned motives could involve financial data theft, the illicit selling of sensitive information, sabotage, intelligence collection, and unlawful wiretapping. Cyberattacks have been a recent result of international political conflict. States facing diplomatic difficulties have been charged with breaking into another nation's computer network in order to obtain private data or carry out sabotage.

Although a cyberattack can take many different forms, its main goals and objectives are to either defame the target or the enterprise or obtain unauthorized access to confidential information. Data collection is the initial stage of a cyberattack. Packet sniffing, document scanning, packet monitoring, and many more techniques can be used to accomplish this. Thus, obtaining private data or vulnerabilities in the network's security is the major goal. Hacking an online resource is one way to obtain information by using the knowledge that has been obtained previously from information collecting. Among the most damaging types of cyberattack, this technique may result in modifications or damage to the data that is stored.

This happens particularly when someone uses deception to obtain passwords or IDs or when they exploit an unattended PC that has a user on it. Following the acquisition of the necessary information, this technique may result in data theft or data interception, two further types of cyberattacks. Attacks that cause an online service to become inaccessible to intended users are known as denial of service attacks. In order to accomplish this, the target is typically overloaded with packets or its resources are depleted to the point where they are permanently lost.

## 2.3 Importance of understanding cyber attacks

Understanding cyber attacks is very important for these reasons listed below:

**I. Prevention:** It is very important to have accurate knowledge of cyber attacks because it allows individuals and organizations to implement preventive measures to safeguard against potential threats. By having proper understanding of how cyber attacks happen, they can protect their systems, networks, and data better.

**II. Detection:** It will be very nice to know and easily recognize the signs of a cyber attack. It will be very helpful for early detection and mitigation. Understanding common attack methods and patterns enables quicker identification of suspicious activities, helping to minimize damage and prevent data breaches.

**III. Response:** For instance, if a cyber attack occurs, knowing how to respond in those circumstances is very important. Accurate understanding of the nature of the attack helps in formulating an appropriate response strategy, including containment, eradication, and recovery procedures.

**IV. Risk Management:** Cyber attacks pose significant risks to individuals, businesses, and governments. Grasping the fundamentals of these risks allows for better risk assessment and management, including the implementation of cybersecurity policies, procedures, and investments.

**V. Legal and Regulatory Compliance:** Many of the top companies and industries have legal and regulatory requirements regarding cybersecurity. Having proper knowledge of cyber attacks helps organizations ensure compliance with relevant laws and regulations, helps to avoid potential fines, penalties, and legal liabilities.

**VI. Business Continuity:** Cyber attacks can disrupt operations and make critical services non functional, this could lead to financial losses and reputational damage. By forecasting a potential impact of cyber attacks on business, most likely it will be negative, contingency plans must be in place, also included should be resilience measures to minimize disruptions.

**VII. Protection of Personal Information:** With the increase of the amount of personal information stored online, understanding cyber attacks is essential for protecting sensitive data from theft, fraud, and misuse. This is very important to help safeguard the individuals' privacy and prevent identity theft.

## 2.4 Types of Cyber Attacks

**I. Phishing Attacks:** This can be done by tricking individuals into providing sensitive information such as passwords or credit card numbers either by disguising as a trustworthy person or entity making use of emails, text message, or other communication channels.

**II. Malware Attacks:** Malware, which stands for malicious software, is a term used to describe viruses, worms, Trojan horses, and other dangerous programs that aim to interfere with, harm, or obtain unauthorized access to computer systems or data.

**III. Denial-of-Service (DoS) and Distributed Denial-of-Service (DDoS) Attacks:** These kinds of attacks aim to overwhelm a system, server, or network with an excessive amount of traffic, making it unavailable for legitimate users to use it.

**IV. Man-in-the-Middle (MitM) Attacks:** In a MitM attack, a cybercriminal eavesdrops on confidential information by intercepting and potentially manipulating communication between two parties.

**V. SQL Injection:** This involves exploiting vulnerabilities in a website or application's database by inserting malicious SQL code, allowing attackers to access, modify, or delete data.

**VI. Ransomware Attacks:** This kind of attack is carried out by locking people out of their computers or encrypting their files, then demanding money (often in cryptocurrency) to unlock them. In this type of extortion, victims are frequently threatened with the disclosure or deletion of their data.

**VII. Social Engineering Attacks:** This is the practice of tricking or manipulating people psychologically in order to coerce them into disclosing private information or taking acts that jeopardize security.

**VIII. Zero-Day Exploits:** This kind of attack targets vulnerabilities in hardware or software that the developer or vendor is unaware of, leaving consumers vulnerable to assaults until a patch or fix is made available.

**IX. Insider Threats:** Insider threats involve individuals within an organization exploiting the access they have with regards to sensitive information for personal gain or to harm the organization.

**X. Advanced Persistent Threats (APTs):** These are state-sponsored entities or well-funded cyber criminal gangs that usually plan elaborate, protracted cyberattacks known as APTs. They do this in order to steal information or interfere with operations, they seek to obtain ongoing access to a network or system.

## 2.5 Cybersecurity measures

The following are some of the cybersecurity measures that individuals and organizations can implement to enhance their security:

**I.Strong Passwords**: You should make it a habit to use complex passwords or passphrases for all accounts, by incorporating a mix of letters, numbers, and special characters.

**II. Multi-Factor Authentication (MFA):** You can enable MFA wherever possible to add that extra layer of security, requiring users of a particular app to provide multiple forms of verification to access accounts or systems.

**III. Regular Software Updates:** Do not slack, continuously keep operating systems, software, and applications up to date with the latest security patches and updates to address vulnerabilities and protect against any eventual exploits.

**IV. Firewalls and Intrusion Detection Systems (IDS):** By implementing firewalls and IDS to help monitor and control incoming and outgoing network traffic, it helps in detecting and blocking suspicious activity or unauthorized access attempts.

**V. Data Encryption:** you can also take more precautions by encrypting sensitive data both in transit and at rest to protect it from unauthorized access or interception. You can use the encryption protocols such as SSL/TLS for web traffic and AES for data storage.

**VI. Security Awareness Training:** It is very important to be able to provide ongoing cybersecurity awareness training for employees to educate them about common threats, phishing scams, and best practices for maintaining security, so that the organization will not be caught unawares.

**VII. Access Controls and Least Privilege:** In order to lower the risk of insider threats and unauthorized access, you can implement access restrictions and adhere to the principle of least privilege, providing users just the permissions necessary to fulfill their responsibilities or tasks.

**VIII. Regular Backups:** There is a need for regular backups of critical and important data and systems to ensure that data can be restored in the event of a cyber attack, ransomware incident, or hardware failure.

**IX. Network Segmentation:** You can segment networks into separate zones or subnetworks with restricted access controls to limit the spread of malware or unauthorized access in the event of a breach.

**X. Penetration Testing and Vulnerability Assessments:** By conducting regular penetration testing and vulnerability assessments we can easily identify and address security weaknesses before they can be exploited by attackers.

### 2.6 Techniques used in cyber attacks

**I. Brute Force Attacks:** In a brute force attack, every password or encryption key combination will be tried until the right one is discovered. Thus unauthorized access to accounts or encrypted data is frequently achieved using this technique.

**II. Cross-Site Scripting (XSS):** Malicious scripts are injected into websites that other users view through XSS attacks, this may compromise their security or steal their personal data. Most of the time attackers leverage on the holes in web apps to install harmful software on consumers' browsers.

### 2.7 Cybersecurity Tools and Technologies

Here is a list of several cybersecurity tools and technologies commonly used in protection against cyber threats:

**I. Firewalls:** These are software programs or security hardware that keep an eye on and regulate all incoming and outgoing network traffic in accordance with pre-established security standards. They support the defense against illegal access to or from private networks.

**II. Anti virus software:** Thus software is used for detecting, preventing, and eliminating malware infections on computers. Real-time protection against viruses, worms, Trojan horses, and other threats is offered by its ability to scan files and programs for recognized malware signatures and behavior patterns.

**III. Intrusion Detection Systems: Systems for detecting intrusions into networks and systems (IDS).** IDS keep an eye out for indications of malicious activity or policy infractions. In order to spot any security incidents and provide alerts for additional research, they examine network traffic, log files, and system events.

**IV. Intrusion Prevention Systems (IPS):** These are advanced security appliances or software solutions that help to monitor network traffic in real-time to detect and block malicious activities. Their function is not only to identify threats but also to take automated actions to prevent them from compromising the network.

**V. Security Information and Event Management (SIEM):** SIEM platforms collect, analyze, and help in correlation of security data from various sources, including logs, sensors, and security devices. They help by providing centralized visibility into security events, which in turn enables faster threat detection, incident response, and compliance management.

**VI. Endpoint Security Solutions:** Endpoint security solutions help to shield laptops, desktops, and mobile devices from online dangers. To protect endpoints both on and off the corporate network, they consist of host-based firewalls, device management features, encryption tools, and antivirus software.

**VII. Data Loss Prevention (DLP):** These solutions prevent sensitive data from being leaked, lost, or stolen by properly monitoring and controlling data transfers across networks, endpoints, and cloud services. They make use of content inspection, encryption, and policy enforcement to be able to safeguard confidential information.

**VIII. Vulnerability Assessment Tools:** This helps to find known security flaws and misconfigurations, vulnerability assessment tools search networks, systems, and apps. If you wish to strengthen overall security posture, they help to pinpoint vulnerabilities that attackers might exploit and offer remedial advice.

**IX. Penetration Testing Tools:** Penetration testing tools are used to examine the security of networks, systems, and applications by simulating cyberattacks. In order to help firms proactively address security threats, they identify potential entry points, vulnerabilities, and flaws that attackers could use.

**X. Identity and Access Management (IAM):** Management of user identities, credentials, and permissions across IT systems and applications is done by Identity and Access Management (IAM) solutions. For you to guarantee that only authorized users have access to resources and data, they implement user provisioning policies, authentication procedures, and access controls.

## 2.8 Encryption Basics

The basic idea in cybersecurity is encryption, which is the process of making use of algorithms and cryptographic keys to transform comprehensible, plaintext data into an encoded format called ciphertext. This procedure makes it hard for people who are not supposed to understand it to comprehend or access the original data without the matching decryption key. For example:

Encryption of plaintext using the Advanced Encryption Standard (AES) algorithm with a cryptographic key:

**Plaintext: Hello, World**

**Key: SecretKey123456**

1.Conversion of plaintext and key to bytes using an encoding scheme (e.g., UTF-8).

- Plaintext bytes: [72, 101, 108, 108, 111, 44, 32, 87, 111, 114, 108, 100, 33]

- Key bytes: [83, 101, 99, 114, 101, 116, 75, 101, 121, 49, 50, 51, 52, 53, 54]

2. You can now apply the AES encryption algorithm with the key.

- The AES encryption process converts plaintext bytes into ciphertext bytes.

3. **Resulting ciphertext (in bytes): [214, 122, 104, 43, 61, 31, 152, 16, 153, 173, 192, 150, 30, 189, 74, 196]**

This ciphertext is the encoded form of the plaintext Hello, World using the AES algorithm and the provided cryptographic key.

There are two main types of encryption: symmetric encryption and asymmetric encryption.

**I.Symmetric Encryption:** In symmetric encryption the same key is used for both encryption and decryption. This implies that the secret key must be safely shared in advance by the sender and the recipient. Data Encryption Standard (DES) and Advanced Encryption Standard (AES) are two examples of symmetric encryption methods.

**II. Asymmetric Encryption**: In asymmetric encryption a public key and a private key are used for encryption and decryption, respectively. While the private key is kept private and is used for decryption, the public key is shared freely and is used for encryption. As a result, the parties involved can communicate securely without exchanging secret keys. Elliptic Curve Cryptography (ECC) and Rivest-Shamir-Adleman (RSA) are two popular asymmetric encryption techniques.

**Rivest-Shamir-Adleman (RSA):** Named after its creators, Ron Rivest, Adi Shamir, and Leonard Adleman, RSA is a popular asymmetric cryptographic technique. It was introduced in 1977. In asymmetric cryptography, two keys are used: a private key for decryption and a public key for encryption. The strength of RSA is its inability to factor two large prime numbers together. Large numbers are thought to be computationally difficult to factor into their prime factors, which is the foundation of RSA's security.

**The RSA algorithm involves the following steps:**

- Key Generation: Two large prime numbers, p and q, are selected, and their product n=p×q is computed. The public key consists of n and another number e (typically a small prime), while the private key consists of n and another number d such that d is the modular multiplicative inverse of e modulo $(p-1) \times (q-1)$.

- **Encryption**: The message is encrypted using the recipient's public key.

- **Decryption**: The ciphertext is decrypted using the recipient's private key.

**Elliptic Curve Cryptography (ECC):** ECC is an additional asymmetric cryptographic procedure that does not rely on integer factorization; rather, it works on elliptic curves over finite fields. With significantly smaller key sizes, ECC provides security comparable to RSA, making it more appropriate for limited contexts like mobile or Internet of Things devices.

The security of ECC is based on the difficulty of the elliptic curve discrete logarithm problem, which involves finding d given Q and k such that $Q = k \times G$, where G is a base point on the elliptic curve and Q is a point resulting from multiplying G by a scalar k.

**The ECC algorithm involves the following steps:**

- **Key Generation**: Similar to RSA, a private key is generated randomly, and a corresponding public key is computed.
- **Encryption:** The message is encrypted using the recipient's public key.

- **Decryption:** The ciphertext is decrypted using the recipient's private key.

Sensitive data is protected by encryption in a variety of activities we do regularly, such as online banking, data storage, and communication. By guaranteeing that only authorized parties can decrypt and retrieve the original material, it helps prevent unauthorized access, eavesdropping, and data breaches. In today's globally interconnected world, encryption is essential to guarantee the secrecy, integrity, and validity of digital information.

## Chapter 3

### 3.1 Securing Personal Devices in cybersecurity

Securing your personal devices is so important in today's tech-driven world. It helps to keep information confidential. These are some of the steps you can take to enhance your cybersecurity:

**I. You can turn on automatic updates:** It is vital for you to regularly update your software (programs, apps, and operating systems) to help fix vulnerabilities and protect against cyber threats. These cybercriminals often exploit coding errors or vulnerabilities in softwares that are outdated. Also, you can enable automatic updates to ensure you receive the latest security patches.

**II. You should activate multi-factor authentication (MFA):** If you use bank accounts for instance, MFA adds an extra layer of security by asking for multiple forms of verification (e.g, password + SMS code) to access your accounts. It will help to keep your accounts safe from cyber attacks. Please try to enable MFA for critical accounts like email, banking, and social media.

**III. Make sure to regularly backup your devices:** You shouldn't for any reason forget to create backups of your important data (documents, photos, etc.) So that you can prevent data loss due to hardware failure, malware, or accidents. You can use cloud storage to do this or external drives for your backups. This is very important.

**IV. Use Passphrases to Secure Your Important Accounts:** You should be very creative with your passwords instead of using simple passwords, you should create strong passphrases with a mix of upper and lower case letters, numbers, and special characters so that your passwords cannot be easily guessed by anyone. It is very important for you to avoid using easily guessable information like birthdays or common words.

**V. You should always secure your mobile device:** Always and don't forget to set a strong PIN, password, or biometric authentication (e.g., fingerprint or face recognition) for your phone.

Make sure you install reputable security apps to scan for malware and protect your device.

**VI. Develop Your Cyber Secure Thinking:** You should be very cautious when clicking on links or downloading attachments in emails or messages. Verify the legitimacy of websites you're clicking on before entering sensitive information. Get current information about common cyber threats and best practices to be on the safe side.

### 3.2 How to secure your home WiFi network

If you wish to secure your home Wi-Fi network, it is very necessary to protect your devices and personal information. Here are some key steps you can take to enhance your Wi-Fi security:

**I. Make sure you encrypt your network:** if there is an encryption it enables the scrambling of the information sent through your network, this makes it harder for others to intercept or access your data. Try to update your router settings to either WPA3 Personal (preferred) or WPA2 Personal encryption. If your router doesn't support WPA3 or WPA2, you can consider upgrading to a newer router for better security.

**II. You should change default settings:** Try and modify the default administrative username, password, and network name (SSID) to unique values. You should avoid the use of login names, passwords, or router brands that anyone can easily guess. You should also reset both the Wi-Fi network password (for device connections) and the router admin password (for administrative access).

**III. Place Your Router Strategically:** You can position your router centrally within your home to ensure better coverage. Do Not place it near windows or external walls, as this can weaken the signal and increase vulnerability.

**IV. Regularly Update Firmware:** Make sure to keep your router's firmware up to date. Manufacturers release updates to fix security vulnerabilities. You can check the manufacturer's website for instructions on updating your specific router model which you use.

**V. Strong Wi-Fi Password:** You must create a strong Wi-Fi password (network key) for connecting devices. You can use a mix of upper and lower case letters, numbers, and special characters. Do Not use common phrases or easily guessable information.

**VI. Firewall and Network Segmentation:** This can enable the router's built-in firewall to filter incoming and outgoing traffic. You should consider segmenting your network by creating a separate guest network for visitors. By doing this it isolates them from your main devices.

**VII. Disable WPS (Wi-Fi Protected Setup):** WPS can be vulnerable to brute-force attacks. You can disable it in your router settings. You can manually enter your Wi-Fi password instead of using WPS.

**VIII. Make sure you monitor Connected Devices:** You should regularly review the list of connected devices in your router settings. You can remove any unknown or unauthorized devices.

**IX. Guest Network:** If your router supports it, you can set up a guest network for visitors. Guests can connect without accessing your main network, enhancing security.

**X. Use MAC Address Filtering**: You can configure your router to allow only specific devices (based on their MAC addresses) to connect. Even though there is no foolproof, it adds an extra layer of control

## 3.3 How to protect yourself from phishing attacks

The term Phishing attacks are a tactic commonly used by cybercriminals to deceive individuals into revealing sensitive information or downloading malware. These are some of the practical steps you can apply to protect yourself:

**I. Make sure you verify the Sender's Identity:** Always do your due diligence by double-checking the sender's authenticity, especially when they are requesting for sensitive information. When you see unexpected emails or messages asking for personal details, be very cautious in providing your details. Don't allow yourself to fall victim.

**II. Use Two-Factor Authentication (2FA):** You can enable 2FA wherever possible. It adds an extra layer of security by prompting for a second form of verification (e.g, SMS code or app-generated token) in addition to the password that you use.

**III. You have to keep Software Updated:** Make sure to regularly update your operating system, applications, and security software. These updates that you do often include patches to fix vulnerabilities that could be exploited by phishing attacks.

**IV. You must use strong passwords**: Do not use passwords anyhow, try to create strong, unique passwords for each account. Try and use a mix of upper and lower case letters, numbers, and special characters. Avoid using information that can be guessed easily like birthdays or common words, this will make it so easy for a phishing attack to occur.

**V. Be Skeptical of Links and Attachments:** When you see links do not just click on them. Do an accurate check over the links to verify their legitimacy before clicking. Don't download attachments from unknown or suspicious sources.

**VI. Educate Yourself and Others:** Try and learn to recognize phishing signs (e.g, misspelled URLs, urgent requests). You can share this knowledge with family and colleagues to prevent them from falling victim.

**VII. Make use of antivirus software:** You can install reputable antivirus software to detect and block any phishing attempts. This antivirus can intercept malicious links before they harm your device.

**VIII. You should Limit putting your personal information online:** You should adjust privacy settings on social media platforms. This will help you to avoid sharing unnecessary personal details that attackers could exploit to cause harm.

**IX. You should continually stay informed:** Try as much as possible to keep up with cybersecurity news and trends. Make up your mind to understand and inundate yourself with evolving phishing techniques to better protect yourself.

## 3.4 Signs of a phishing email

For you to spot phishing emails it could be a tricky exercise, but if you're observant there are several telltale signs you can watch out for. Here i listed ten common indicators that an email might be a phishing attempt:

**I. If the email has an unfamiliar tone or greeting:** you should pay attention to the language used in conveying the email. If it feels off for example, maybe a colleague being overly familiar or a family member sounding too formal in the mail, it could be a serious red flag.

**II. If it has grammar and spelling errors:** Though it might not always be present, but note that mistakes in grammar and spelling are the common characteristics in phishing emails. Cybercriminals often rush their messages, leading to spelling errors.

**III. You can dictate this by the urgency or threats:** Most phishing emails often create a sense of urgency or fear. They might tell you that your account will be suspended or blocked, or they'll tell you you'll face legal consequences if you don't act immediately and be very observant with all these.

**IV. It has a generic greeting or lack of personalization:** Be alert because of emails that start with generic greetings like **"Dear Customer"** instead of using your name. If a legitimate organization wants to write to you or they want to pass information to you they usually personalize their communications.

## 3.5 Firewalls in cybersecurity

A firewall is a network security device that acts as a protective barrier between your computer network and external networks (such as the internet). The primary purpose of a firewall is to monitor and control incoming and outgoing traffic, allowing authorized traffic while at the same blocking unwanted or malicious traffic. Notably you can also think of it as a digital gatekeeper that helps in filtering data packets attempting to enter or exit your network.

**How Firewalls Works**

Firewalls operate by following a predefined set of security rules and procedures:

When data packets arrive at the firewall, the major function of the firewall is to inspect them based on these rules. If for instance the content meets the specified criteria (e.g, matches allowed protocols, IP addresses, or port numbers), the firewall will permit it. On the contrary it does not permit it, it blocks or rejects the traffic.

**Firewalls can be deployed in various ways**

- **Hardware Appliances:** This is a dedicated device placed at the network perimeter.
- **Software Firewalls:** This is installed on individual computers or servers.
- **Software as a Service (SaaS):** This is a cloud-based firewalls.

**Types of Firewalls**

**I. Stateless or Packet Filtering Firewall:** This helps to examine individual packets of data without considering their context. Thus decisions are always based on predefined rules for each packet.

**II. Stateful Inspection Firewall:** This is more sophisticated than stateless firewalls. It helps to maintain a state table, and also helps in tracking the state of active connections. It also considers the context of packets (e.g, whether they belong to an established connection) for better decision making.

**III. Circuit-Level Gateway:** This works well at the transport layer (OSI Layer 4). It helps authenticate and validate connections between hosts.

**IV. Application-Level Gateway (Proxy Firewall):** This mostly operates at the application layer (OSI Layer 7). It also acts as an intermediary between clients and servers. This application helps to provide deep inspection of application specific traffic.

**V. Next-Generation Firewall (NGFW):** This combines traditional firewall features with intrusion prevention, application awareness, and more. It also offers advanced threat detection and prevention too.

**The role of firewalls in cybersecurity**

Firewalls play a very important role in cybersecurity by acting as a protective barrier between a particular organization's internal network and external networks. Let us look at their significance or importance:

**I. Helps for network segregation:** Firewalls enable the formation of boundaries between secured internal networks and untrusted external networks. They help to create barriers, thereby preventing unauthorized access to private data and sensitive systems.

**II. Traffic Control and Validation:** Firewalls serve as traffic controllers, managing and validating network access. Helps in monitoring incoming and outgoing data packets based on predetermined security rules. It has to be only trusted sources and IP addresses that are allowed to access the organization's systems.

**III. Web Traffic Filtering:** Firewalls help to build checkpoints to filter web traffic. By analysis of data packets, they can help to identify and act upon rogue network traffic before any adverse effects occur. This protection procedure minimizes the spread of web threats.

**IV. Intrusion Prevention:** Firewalls equipped with an integrated intrusion prevention system (IPS) can help to block malware and application layer attacks. Firewalls can swiftly detect and respond to attacks throughout the network.

**V. Protection Against Vulnerabilities:** If a network is lacking proper protection they are vulnerable to attacks. Thus firewalls help to vet network traffic, by helping to distinguish between harmful from benign connections. As a user for instance who connects personal devices to the internet that individual risks the exposure to various threats. Firewalls help to mitigate the risk of hacking, identity theft, and online fraud by providing a higher degree of safety while surfing the internet.

## 3.6 Protecting Your Computer

Protection of your computer in cybersecurity involves the implementation of various measures to safeguard your system, data, and privacy from unauthorized access, theft, or damage. Here's a list of what to do to achieve this:

**I.Installation and Updating of Antivirus Software**: when antivirus software is installed it helps to detect and remove malicious programs like viruses, worms, and Trojans. It will be very useful and helpful too if you can regularly update your antivirus software to ensure it can detect the latest threats.

**II. Enabling of Firewall Protection:** A firewall acts as a barrier between your computer and external networks, monitoring and controlling incoming and outgoing traffic. It gives enablement in the built-in firewall on your operating system or install a third-party firewall for added protection.

**III. Keep Software Updated:** you should regularly update your operating system, web browsers, and applications to patch security vulnerabilities. Cybercriminals often exploit outdated software to gain access to computers.

**IV. Usage of strong passwords**: you can create strong, unique passwords for your accounts and change them regularly. You should avoid using easily guessable passwords like **password or 123456.** You should consider using a password manager to securely store and manage your passwords.

**V. You should enable two-factor authentication (2FA):** 2FA adds that extra layer of security by requiring users to provide a second form of authentication, such as a code sent to their mobile device, in addition to their password.

**VI. Be extremely cautious of phishing attacks:** people tend to use phishing emails and websites in an attempt to trick users into providing sensitive information like login credentials or financial details. Be cautious of unsolicited emails, and make sure you verify the authenticity of websites before inputting any of your personal information.

**VII. Make sure you backup your data regularly:** you should regularly backup your important files and data to an external hard drive, cloud storage service, or a backup server. In the event of a cyber attack or hardware failure, you can easily restore your data from the backup.

**VIII. Make sure to encrypt your data:** Encryption helps in scrambling data to make it unreadable without the proper decryption key. You can use encryption tools to encrypt sensitive files, folders, and communications so as to prevent unauthorized access.

**IX. Limit User Privileges:** try to restrict user privileges to prevent unauthorized users or malware from making system changes. Make sure to use standard user accounts for everyday tasks and also reserve administrator privileges for system maintenance and updates.

**X. Educating Yourself and Others**: always stay informed about the latest cybersecurity threats and best practices. Give yourself to education and even others in your household or workplace about adhering to safe computing habits and how to recognize potential security risks.

### 3.7 Safe Browsing Practices

Here are 10 safe browsing practices to follow in cybersecurity:

**I. Verify Website URLs:** Before you enter any sensitive information or make online purchases, you should double check the URL to ensure it begins with **"https://"** and includes a padlock icon, indicating a secure connection.

**II. Use Ad Blockers:** you should consider using ad blockers to prevent malicious ads from appearing on websites you visit. Malvertising (malicious advertising) can lead to malware infections or phishing attempts.

**III. Update Web Browser and Plugins**: make sure you keep your web browser and plugins (such as Flash Player and Java) up to date with the latest security patches and updates so that it can minimize vulnerabilities that could be exploited by attackers.

**IV. Clear your browser cache and cookies:** make sure you regularly clear your browser cache and cookies for the removal of temporary files and tracking data that could be used to monitor your online activities or compromise your privacy.

**V. Enable Browser Security Features:** Take advantage of built-in browser security features such as pop-up blockers, phishing protection, and safe browsing modes to help protect against malicious websites and downloads.

**VI. Use Strong Privacy Settings:** you can adjust your browser's privacy settings to limit the amount of information websites can collect about you, such as location data, browsing history, and cookies.

**VI. Avoid Public Wi-Fi for Sensitive Activities:** you can avoid accessing sensitive information, such as online banking or shopping, while connected to public Wi-Fi networks. If necessary, use a virtual private network (VPN) to encrypt your internet traffic.

**VII. Regularly Scan for Malware:** you can use a set of reputable antivirus and anti-malware software to regularly scan your computer for malicious programs or files that could compromise your security while browsing the web.

If you can follow these safe browsing practices, you can minimize the risks of encountering malware, phishing attempts, and other online threats while making use of the web.

# Chapter 4

## 4.1 Securing Internet of Things (IoT) Devices

When we have a discourse about securing Internet of Things (IoT) devices in cybersecurity, this is very important due to the growing number of interconnected devices, ranging from smart home appliances to industrial machinery. There should be Implementation of strong authentic mechanisms to ensure that only authorized users or devices can access the IoT system. This entails using secure protocols such as OAuth or OpenID Connect to manage the credentials securely. The encryption of data both at rest and in transit for the protection from unauthorized access. This includes the usage of protocols like TLS (Transport Layer Security) for secure communication between devices and servers, as well as encryption algorithms to protect already stored data. You can regularly update IoT device firmware and software so as to address already known vulnerabilities and security flaws. This will require establishing a robust patch management process that will help in ensuring timely updates without the disruption of device functionality.

The segregation of IoT devices onto separate networks or VLANs (Virtual Local Area Networks) to minimize the potential impact of a security breach, helps to contain threats and also prevents attackers from easily moving laterally across the network. The use of strong authentication mechanisms, such as biometric authentication or multi-factor authentication, is to ensure that only authorized users can access IoT devices. There could also be the implementation of granular access controls to limit the privileges of each user or device. Therefore adherence to secure coding practices when developing IoT devices and applications to minimize the risk of introducing vulnerabilities includes performing security testing, code reviews, and implementing secure coding guidelines such as the ones already outlined by OWASP (Open Web Application Security Project). There is also the protection of physical access to IoT devices that helps to prevent tampering or unauthorized access. This entails implementing physical security measures such as locks, tamper evident seals, and secure mounting of devices.

When we Implement robust monitoring and logging mechanisms it helps us to detect and respond to security incidents in real-time, monitoring network traffic, device behavior, and system logs for signs of suspicious activity or unauthorized access. You can also assess the security posture of IoT device vendors and suppliers to ensure they follow the right practices for security and privacy. This will include evaluating their security certifications, adherence to industry standards, and commitment to ongoing security updates and support. It's also very important to be provided guidance on password hygiene, recognizing phishing attempts, and reporting suspicious activity in real time. With all these in mind. By addressing these aspects comprehensively, organizations can enhance the security of IoT devices and reduce the risks associated with their widespread adoption in various industries.

## 4.2 Introduction to Cyber Hygiene

The actions and procedures people and organizations use in upholding sound cybersecurity policies and defending themselves against online threats are collectively referred to as cyber hygiene. It is comparable to good personal hygiene in the real world, where consistent practices like brushing your teeth and washing your hands help keep you healthy and free from illness. Comparably, maintaining cyber hygiene is taking regular precautions against online threats to protect systems, data, and digital assets. The value of awareness and education is one of the core components of cyber hygiene. Gaining knowledge about prevalent cyber hazards, like malware infections, phishing scams, and social engineering techniques, enables people and businesses to identify and reduce possible risks. Users could make more educated decisions and take proactive measures to safeguard themselves and their digital assets by keeping up to date with the latest cybersecurity trends and best practices.

Very importantly, maintaining good cyber hygiene requires diligence and consistency. It's not enough to implement security measures once and forget about them, no it should not be that way rather, it is supposed to be an ongoing process that requires regular attention and updates. Just as we brush our teeth every day to prevent cavities, we must regularly update software, back up important data, and review security settings to prevent cyber incidents. Using technology to improve security is an important component of cyber hygiene.

Protection against cyber risks and preventing unwanted access to sensitive information are made possible by tools like firewalls, encryption, and antivirus software. All technology, though, is not enough, it needs to be combined with responsible behavior and human judgment. We must use caution online so that we can prevent becoming victims of cyberattacks, just as we rely on common sense and deep thinking to keep secure in the real world.

Additionally, communities and organizations should also be accountable for practicing cyber hygiene. Establishing cybersecurity standards and encouraging collaboration in the fight against cyber threats are responsibilities of governments and international organizations, while businesses must have strong cybersecurity policies and processes in place to safeguard their resources and customer data.

### 4.3 Benefits of Cyber Hygiene

**I. Maintenance**: if you can maintain a good online hygiene it will enable your software and PCs to function at their peak. Updating your system's software and preventing vulnerabilities both assist in preventing cyber attacks.

**II. Security:** This is the most important part. Practices related to cyber hygiene equip you to combat viruses, malware, hackers, and identity thieves. You lower your risk of cyber dangers by taking preemptive measures.

**III. Helps to Improve system performance:** If you keep systems updated and free of malware, cyber hygiene ensures that devices and networks operate efficiently, minimizing downtime and disruptions or it might even be non-existent especially when you're making use of the internet or systems.

**IV. Helps in the protection of Sensitive Information**: Strict adherence to cyber hygiene practices helps in safeguarding sensitive data such as personal, financial, and business information from being compromised or stolen.

**V. Helps in the preservation of Reputation:** if you maintain good cyber hygiene it reflects positively on individuals and organizations, it helps to foster trust among customers, partners, and stakeholders.

**VI. Compliance with Regulations:** Following cyber hygiene protocols ensures compliance with industry standards and regulations, avoiding potential legal consequences and financial penalties.

### 4.4 Common Cyber Hygiene Problems

A lot of enterprises deal with various elements that require cyber hygiene:

- **Hardware**: Computers, phones, and connected devices.
- **Software Programs**: Regular updates and patches are essential and very important
- **Online Applications**: Always ensure they're secure, don't release any personal information that can be used against you.

**Problems include:**

- **Loss of Data:** if there is unmaintained hard drives and cloud storage, it can lead to data loss due to hacking or corruption.
- **Misplaced Data:** if there are so many places to store data, files can easily get misplaced.

### 4.5 Regular Software Updates

Why Software Updates is so important:

Our computers, tablets, and phones are devices we might not do without, it helps us to store a wealth of information about our online activities, personal data, and financial details. However, even though these gadgets help us enormously they also expose us to cyber threats. Hackers constantly search for vulnerabilities in software to exploit.

Operating systems (OS) manage all the functionality on your computer. They have built-in functions to prevent attacks. The challenge is that cyber threats evolve continuously. To stay ahead, OS providers release regular updates to tackle changing threats from cybercriminals. If you neglect OS updates, you are at the risk of losing data or compromising access to very important accounts, potentially costing you your identity and money.

**How Software Updates Protect You:**

If you can regularly update your OS it is one of the simplest ways to thwart cybercriminals attempting to steal your information.

These updates include:
- **Security Patches**: Fix vulnerabilities that hackers could exploit.
- **Bug Fixes:** make sure to address glitches and improve system stability.
- Make sure you keep your OS up-to-date, you strengthen your defense against cyberattacks.

**Tricks for Remembering to Update Your Software:**

- **Enable automatic updates yourself:** Most operating systems (for both mobile devices and personal computers) offer automatic download and installation of updates. Once enabled, your OS will automatically apply key cybersecurity fixes as soon as they're available.

- **Avoid opening your device at off hours:** You should avoid updating software when you're in the middle of a task. Software updates often require your device to be temporarily unavailable and may necessitate you to restart your computer, or phone. You should be able to set aside time during off-hours to allow updates to complete and not disrupt your work or personal tasks as a result of the updates.

### 4.6 Data Backup Practices

Imagine if you're diligently working on an important project, and suddenly your computer crashes. Panic sets in as you realize that your important files are gone.

Loss of data can occur due to various reasons:

- **Human error:** spilling liquid on your keyboard can cause it, accidental deletion can cause it too, or maybe you forgot to save files securely.
- **Hard drive failures**: when hard drives are aging it can cause it, also exposure to magnetic fields, overheating, and other factors.
- **Computer malware:** statistics show that up to 30% of U.S. computers are infected by malware, which can corrupt data or lead to ransomware attacks.

**The Basics of Data Backups:**

Backing up data means duplication of copies of that data. It also involves creating copies of information stored on your devices (desktops, laptops, smartphones, tablets).

What to backup are as follows:

- Documents, photos, emails, address books, videos, machine images, operating systems, and registry files. The goal and objective of this is to deposit your data in a separate, secure location away from your devices for easy retrieval when needed.

**The 3-2-1 Backup Strategy:**

The 3-2-1 backup strategy means having:
- At least three copies of your data,
- That is stored on two different types of media, and
- One copy stored offsite or in the cloud.

You can always follow this strategy to increase the likelihood of successful data duplication and recovery:

**Two storage types:**
- You can use different storage media (e.g., external hard drives, cloud storage).

**One copy can be stored offsite:**
- You can store away from your home or business (in case of disasters).

**The Best Practices for Data Backups:**

- Always back up your data consistently, don't wait until disaster strikes before you think of backing your files up.
- You can enable automatic backups whenever possible.
- **Immutable Backups:** you can also create at least one copy that cannot be altered. It will help you massively(air-gapped backups).
- You can periodically restore data from backups to ensure they work effectively and you're not taking chances.
- **Offsite Storage:** you can use cloud services or physically store backups away from your primary location.

# Chapter 5

## 5.1 Cybersecurity Best Practices for Businesses

Cybersecurity best practices for businesses are very important in the protection of sensitive information, it helps in the maintenance of customer trust, and prevents costly data breaches. You can begin by conducting a thorough assessment of your business's cybersecurity risks. After you've conducted this assessment you should be able to Identify potential vulnerabilities in your systems, networks, and processes. These assessments will help you to carve out niches on how to handle cyber attacks. You can also develop a comprehensive cybersecurity policy outlining guidelines, procedures, and protocols that employees should follow. There is a need to educate your employees about cybersecurity risks and best practices. It is very important to train them on how to recognize phishing emails, avoid clicking on suspicious links, and report any security incidents promptly.

Make sure you regularly backup important data and systems to secure offsite locations. In the event of a ransomware attack or data breach, having up-to-date backups can minimize downtime and data loss. Create a thorough incident response strategy that specifies what should be done in the event of a cybersecurity problem. You can assign team members duties and responsibilities and set up procedures for communicating with stakeholders. You should assess the security procedures followed by outside service providers and vendors who have access to your data or systems. To reduce possible dangers, make sure they abide by industry norms and laws. To properly evaluate the efficacy of your security controls and find any vulnerabilities or openings that require attention, you must conduct routine cybersecurity audits. You have to keep up with the latest information on industry-specific cybersecurity laws and regulations. Make sure that the rules and standards that apply to your cybersecurity activities are followed.

## 5.2 Employee Training and Awareness

A successful cybersecurity strategy for firms must include employee awareness and training. A thorough understanding of cybersecurity risks is essential for staff members. These risks include social engineering, malware infections, phishing scams, and insider threats. Employees can safeguard firm assets with greater diligence and initiative if they are aware of these hazards. Phishing emails can be identified because fraudsters frequently use them to deceive people into disclosing personal information or downloading hazardous malware. Staff members ought to receive training on identifying phishing emails by scanning for warning signs such dubious sender addresses, pressing wording, and requests for private data. It is very important that employees receive training on safe internet browsing techniques in order to prevent them from unintentionally visiting hazardous websites or downloading harmful content. This involves being cautious while obtaining data from unidentified sources and refraining from clicking on dubious links or advertisements.

Workers should get training on how to make complicated passwords, steer clear of using the same password for several accounts, and, when feasible, implement multi-factor authentication. Workers must be aware of the significance of handling and safeguarding sensitive data with care. To prevent information from being kept longer than necessary, this entails safely storing data, encrypting files when needed, and adhering to data retention policies. Employee education should focus on the significance of device security, including for PCs, laptops, tablets, and cellphones. Activating device encryption, updating operating systems and apps, and installing antivirus software are all examples of this.

Employees should be able to quickly notify the relevant IT or security staff about any security incidents or suspicious conduct. The impact of security incidents can be lessened and more harm to the company can be avoided with prompt reporting. Training of employees should be a continuous process because cyber threats are always changing. To guarantee that staff members are up to date on the newest cybersecurity dangers and recommended procedures, regular training sessions and updates should be given. Assuring that cybersecurity stays a primary concern for all staff members requires developing a culture of security awareness throughout the company. A sense of shared responsibility for safeguarding corporate assets is fostered, open discussion about security concerns is encouraged, and employees who exhibit effective security practices are acknowledged and rewarded.

## 5.3 Incident Response and Recovery

In cybersecurity, incident response and recovery relate to the systems and protocols implemented to efficiently handle and lessen the effects of security incidents, such as hacks, data breaches, and compromised systems. Detecting, evaluating, and quickly responding to security issues are all part of incident response. Usually, an organized methodology is used, comprising:

**I.Identifying and Detecting**: Keeping an eye out for indicators of questionable behavior or security lapses, like anomalous network traffic patterns or unauthorized access attempts, on systems and networks.

**II. Eradication and containment:** Prevention of more harm or unwanted access by isolating compromised systems or networks. Patching vulnerabilities, eliminating malware, and deactivating hacked accounts might all be part of this.

**III.** Determining the incident's extent, significance, and underlying reasons through investigation is known as forensic analysis. This entails gathering and examining digital evidence, logs, and artifacts in order to determine the strategies, means, and intents of the attacker.

**IV.** Informing all parties involved on the incident's status, consequences, and measures to restore it through communication and notification. As mandated by relevant laws and regulations, this involves informing impacted parties, such as clients, staff members, lawmakers, or law enforcement organizations.

V. Recovering and correcting the situation involves both putting the impacted systems or services back in order and taking steps to make sure that something similar doesn't happen again. Applying security patches, enhancing security controls and processes, or recovering data from backups could all be part of this.

**Recovery**

Recovery is the process of getting impacted systems, data, and services back to normal after a security incident. Data recovery is the process of restoring damaged or lost data from backups or other sources in order to prevent further data loss and maintain company operations. System restoration is the process of reconstructing or rearranging infrastructure or systems that have been compromised in order to get rid of any malicious malware or unauthorized access. Restoring affected services or applications to their regular state in order to reduce downtime and preserve company operations is known as service restoration. Reviewing or learning from an occurrence to assess how well incident response protocols are working, pinpoint areas that need work, and make necessary updates to security rules, controls, or training.

## 5.4 Steps to take after a security breach

In order to lessen the effects and stop additional harm after a security compromise, quick action is needed. The steps to follow are as follows:

**I.** You should stop the breach from spreading further by quickly isolating the compromised systems or networks. This could include removing hacked devices from the network, restricting harmful traffic, and deactivating hacked accounts.

**II. Evaluate:** You can evaluate the extent and seriousness of the hack to find out which systems or data have been affected and how the attack happened. By finding the primary cause and any vulnerabilities that were exploited, you must do a comprehensive investigation.

**III. Notification:** you can advise senior management, internal teams, legal counsel, and, if necessary, regulatory agencies, clients, and partners of the breach. To keep people's trust and make a coordinated reaction possible, transparency is essential.

**IV. Maintain Digital Evidence:** Try to keep track of network traffic information, system snapshots, logs, and other digital evidence connected to the incident. Forensic investigation, event reaction, and prospective legal actions will all require this information.

**V. Corrective action:** make sure to take prompt corrective action to fix the vulnerabilities that were taken advantage of during the incident. Changing compromised passwords, applying security patches, upgrading security configurations, and implementing extra security measures are a few possible solutions for this.

**VI.** Maintain open lines of communication with all parties involved regarding the status of cleanup operations and any modifications to security protocols. In order to respond to inquiries, grievances, and comments from impacted parties, you must establish clear lines of communication.

**VII.** Keep an eye out for any indications of current or upcoming assaults by regularly monitoring systems and networks. Install security information and event management (SIEM) programs, intrusion detection systems, and other monitoring tools to quickly identify and address suspicious activity.

**VIII.** You can conduct a thorough post-incident review to analyze the effectiveness of the response and identify areas for improvement.

Make sure you document lessons learned, update incident response procedures, and implement any necessary changes to strengthen the organization's security posture.

## 5.5 Data Recovery Techniques

These are methods for recovering lost, corrupted, or unreadable data from storage devices such as memory cards, USB drives, solid-state drives (SSDs), and hard drives are known as data recovery techniques. In the event of data corruption, formatting errors, hardware malfunctions, or inadvertent deletion, these methods are very important for retrieving important information. The following are a few methods for data recovery:

**I. File System Reconstruction**: To locate and restore deleted or lost files, file system reconstruction entails examining the file system architecture of a storage device. To find and recreate file entries, this method depends on knowledge of the file allocation table (FAT), master file table (MFT), or other file system metadata.

**II.** The process of searching through unprocessed data on a storage device for particular file signatures or patterns linked to frequently used file types—such as JPEG for images and DOCX for documents—is called data carving, sometimes referred to as file carving or file recovery by signature. Partially erased or fragmented files can be recovered with this technique.

**III. Disk Imaging:** This process entails making an exact replica of a storage device, complete with all of its data and file structures. Data recovery software can then be used to examine and process this image in order to retrieve specific files or directories, regardless of whether the original device is broken or unusable.

**IV.** The process of recreating a RAID array following the failure of one or more disks is known as RAID reconstruction, or **redundant array of independent disks**. To recover lost or unreachable data, this may entail swapping out failing drives, reconstructing parity data, and reestablishing data redundancy.

**V.** To get data from a storage device remotely, one must use a network connection to access and retrieve the data. Using this method is common when working with distant servers or cloud-based storage, or when there is no way to physically touch the device.

**VI.** Repairing or replacing damaged components, such as read/write heads, circuit boards, or drive motors, may be necessary for data recovery in situations when data loss is the result of physical harm or mechanical malfunction. Specialized equipment and methods carried out in a cleanroom setting could be required for this.

**VII. Data Duplication:** If you want to make a backup or maintain data integrity while recovering from an error, you may want to transfer data from one storage device to another. Retrying the recovery process in the event that it is unsuccessful guarantees that the original data stays unaltered.

**VIII. Data Backup Restoration:** Recovering data from a backup can sometimes be the most straightforward step in the process. One of the best ways to retrieve lost data is to regularly backup important/sensitive files and data to network servers, external storage devices, or cloud-based services. By using these data recovery methods, people and organizations can lessen the effects of data loss occurrences and improve their chances of recovering lost or inaccessible data.

# Chapter 6

## 6.1 Emerging Trends in Cybersecurity

Here are some of the emerging trends in cybersecurity:

**I. Zero Trust Architecture:** This strategy places a strong emphasis on rigorous identity verification for any individual or device attempting to access network resources, whether they are located inside or outside the perimeter.

**What is Zero Trust?**

Zero Trust is a security framework that challenges the conventional perimeter-based security model. It assumes that there is no longer a clear network edge due to the proliferation of remote work, cloud services, and hybrid environments. Everyone who uses the network of the company, whether they are inside or not, is viewed in suspicion as a zero trust paradigm. Before they may access apps and data, they need to be properly approved, authenticated, and confirmed throughout. The core principle of Zero Trust is **"never to trust, and always verify."**

**Key Principles of Zero Trust:**

- **Continuous Verification:** it's very necessary to always verify access, all the time, for all resources. This could involve ongoing validation of user identity, their security configuration, and posture.

- **Limiting the "Blast Radius":** it helps by minimizing the impact if an external or insider breach occurs. This is done by segmenting access and enforcing least privilege, this helps the damage that could be caused by a compromised account to be limited.

- **Automate Context Collection and Response:** you can gather context from the entire IT stack (identity, endpoint, workload, etc.) to provide accurate responses. Behavioral data helps one to make informed decision making.

**Components of Zero Trust:**

- **Risk-Based Multi-Factor Authentication (MFA):** this helps to ensure a strong authentication based on risk factors.

- **Identity Protection:** this helps to safeguard user identities and prevents unauthorized access.

- **Next-Generation Endpoint Security:** this protects endpoints from threats.

- **Cloud Workload Security:** this ensures security for resources in the cloud.

**NIST 800-207 and Zero Trust:** It is widely acknowledged that the NIST 800-207 standard provides an extensive set of guidelines for the implementation of Zero Trust. It talks about concepts like context-aware answers and ongoing verification. Thus, private organizations see it as the accepted norm for the implementation of Zero Trust. U.S. Federal Agencies are required by the Biden administration to follow NIST 800-207 for Zero Trust implementation.

**Why Zero Trust Matters:**

- **Securing Remote Workers**: Zero Trust accommodates the rise of remote work and also protects them by focusing on user behavior and context. Securing remote workers involves implementing measures to protect the devices, data, and communications of employees who work outside of traditional office environments. This entails making certain that the security software on the devices used by remote workers is up to date, using secure networks like VPNs to allow remote access to company resources, enforcing multi-factor authentication and other strong authentication techniques, and training staff members on cybersecurity best practices. In order to reduce the possible security risks connected with remote work, companies can also use zero trust to manage and monitor remote devices in addition to putting policies and processes for data protection and incident response into place.

- **Hybrid Cloud Environments**: It adapts to the dynamic nature of cloud resources. A hybrid cloud environment refers to a computing infrastructure that combines elements of both public and private clouds, allowing data and applications to be shared between them seamlessly. Through their on-premises or private cloud infrastructure, businesses may retain control over sensitive data and vital apps while also taking advantage of the scalability and affordability of public cloud services. Businesses can meet changing workload demands, optimize resources, and comply with security and compliance regulations because of the flexibility this hybrid strategy affords.

- **Ransomware Threats:** Ransomware threats involve malicious software that encrypts files or locks users out of their systems, demanding payment (a "ransom") in exchange for restoring access. Zero Trust mitigates the impact of breaches

## 6.2 How to implement Zero Trust in your organization

Implementing Zero Trust Architecture (ZTA) in your organization involves several steps, it is listed and explained below:

- **Identify Sensitive Assets:** You can begin by identifying the most important data, applications, and resources that need protection. Also it's very essential to understand what you want to safeguard and where it resides.

- **Map Data Flow and Access:** Give a proper analysis of how information flows within your organization. Make sure you identify who accessed what, from where, and under what circumstances. Put in consideration both internal and external users, including remote workers and third-party partners.

- **Define Micro Perimeters:** Zero Trust relies on micro-segmentation. That means Dividing your network into smaller segments or zones based on the sensitivity of data. Then by Creating access boundaries around these segments, allowing only authorized traffic.

- **Implement Access Controls**: make use of network access Control (NAC) systems to enforce policies. These systems verify user and device authenticity before granting access.

- **Least privilege is so important:** Users and devices should only have permissions necessary for their tasks.

- **Multi-Factor Authentication (MFA):** for improvement in authentication, use multi-factor authentication (MFA). It increases security by requiring two or more types of verification. Think about elements such as the user's knowledge (password), possessions (token), and identity (biometrics).

- **Endpoint Security:** To ensure robust security for endpoints (devices). You should make use of the next-generation endpoint protection tools. Regularly/continuously check and validate the security posture of devices before you grant access.

- **Behavioral Analytics and Context:** Collect context from the entire IT stack (identity, endpoint, workload, etc.). Use the behavioral pattern of data to make informed and precise decisions and respond accurately.

- **Secure Email and Data Encryption:** Make sure there is encryption of sensitive data in transit and at rest. Also Implement secure email gateways for the prevention of phishing attacks.

- **Collaboration Across Teams:** In zero trust, it is a necessity for collaboration between IT, security, and business units.

Doing this defines the roles, the responsibilities, and the communication channels.

- **Continuous Monitoring and Adaptation:** Zero Trust is not something you set up and say you've done it all, there still needs to be Continuous monitoring and adaptations to trends or whatsoever in cybersecurity. There should be regular review of access policies, adjust micro perimeters, and stay concurrently informed about threats.

## 6.3 How to handle legacy systems within a Zero Trust framework

Although integrating legacy systems into a Zero Trust framework can be a little bit difficult, doing so is necessary for a thorough security strategy. Let us look at some strategies which could be employed to achieve this:

- **Assess Your Legacy Systems:** You can begin by identifying the legacy systems in your environment. Understand their architecture, dependencies, and limitations. You must evaluate their compatibility with Zero Trust principles. Some legacy systems may lack necessary features or may be difficult to modify.

- **Segmentation and Micro Perimeters:** You must segment your network based on sensitivity. Establish small boundaries around vital resources, such as old systems. Keep legacy systems' and other network segments' communication to a minimum. To enforce policies, use network access controls.

**Gradual Transition:**
- **Phased approach:** take it easy and migrate gradually. Do not attempt to overhaul all legacy systems at once.
- **Prioritize:** you should focus on important legacy applications first. Also considering their business impact and risk impact too.

- **Proxy and Gateway Solutions:** Before outdated systems, put in place identity-aware proxies or gateways. In accordance with Zero Trust guidelines, these proxies are capable of managing traffic filtering, authorization, and authentication.

- **Authentication and Authorization:** This enhances authentication for legacy systems. Make sure you Implement multi-factor authentication (MFA) where possible.

- **Behavioral Monitoring:** you should deploy behavioral analytics tools to enable monitoring legacy system activity. It helps to detect anomalies, unauthorized access, or suspicious behavior.

- **Secure Communication Channels:** You can encrypt communication between legacy systems and other components to enable prevention of an attack. You should use secure protocols to prevent eavesdropping.

- **Legacy System Hygiene:** Give outdated systems regular updates and patches. Address weaknesses as soon as possible. Eliminate any pointless accounts and services.

- **Vendor Support and Modernization:** Talk to the providers of older systems. Find out about any fixes or security upgrades. Look at ways to gradually replace or modernize outdated systems.

- **Documentation and Training:** Keep track of historical system configurations, policies, and access restrictions. Employees should receive training on Secure Legacy Component handling and Zero Trust principles.

**II. Cloud Security:** Data storage and transmission security in the cloud has become a major concern due to the extensive use of cloud services. Increasingly popular solutions include encryption and cloud access security brokers (CASBs).

**III. IoT Security:** Since many Internet of Things (IoT) devices are low-powered and lack strong security features, the growth of IoT devices presents new cybersecurity concerns. It is very important to secure IoT networks and devices to stop them from being used as gateways into more complex systems.

**IV. Ransomware Protection:** The persistent evolution of ransomware assaults presents a substantial risk to enterprises of varying magnitudes. Thus, in order to reduce the likelihood of successful ransomware attacks, more attention needs to be paid to developing strong backup and recovery solutions as well as enhancing employee awareness and training.

**V. Endpoint Security:** Endpoint security has never been more important than it is now, with the growth of remote work and the proliferation of connected devices. To be able to identify and counteract attacks that target endpoints, such as laptops, cellphones, and tablets, solutions like endpoint detection and response (EDR) are being used.

**What Is Endpoint Security?**

The practice of defending workstations, servers, and other devices (that can accept a security client) against malevolent threats and cyberattacks is known as endpoint security. Businesses can use it to safeguard servers located on a network or on the cloud, as well as endpoints used by staff members for work-related activities. The following are the key aspects of endpoint security:

**Endpoint Types:**

- **Workstations**: These include desktops, laptops, and mobile devices that are mostly used by employees.
- **Servers:** these are very important systems that store and manage data, applications, and services.
- **Other Devices:** comprises printers, IoT devices, and any network-connected hardware.

## Challenges of endpoint Security:

Cybercriminals with advanced skills are posing a growing danger to the cybersecurity of modern businesses. Because of their enormous quantity and function in network connectivity, endpoints are frequently targeted. Thus, securing endpoints becomes more challenging due to legacy technology and a variety of device kinds.

- **Diverse Endpoints**: Due to differences in operating systems, apps, and patch levels, managing security across a variety of endpoint devices, including laptops, smartphones, and Internet of Things devices, can be difficult.

- **Remote Workforce**: As remote work becomes more common, it is essential to secure endpoints outside of the conventional corporate network perimeter. This calls for strong solutions that can fend off threats coming from various networks and locales.

- **Zero-Day Exploits:** It is especially difficult to fight against zero-day attacks since they target vulnerabilities that the vendor is unaware of. Preemptively identifying and addressing these risks before they may be used is very important for endpoint security solutions.

- **User Awareness and Behavior:** When users click on malicious links or download infected files, for example, endpoints will be definitely compromised. It's important **"yes"** but difficult to enforce policies to stop risky activity and to teach people about security best practices.

- **Evolving Threat Landscape:** Attackers have found a way to make use of advanced strategies to get around conventional endpoint security measures, and cyber dangers are always changing. Threat information, constant monitoring, and frequent security solution updates are all necessary to stay ahead of these always changing threats.

**Benefits of Endpoint Security:**

- **Threat Detection and Prevention:** In order to protect endpoints from compromise, endpoint security solutions identify and stop a variety of threats, including ransomware, malware, and phishing attempts.

- **Data Protection:** Encryption, access limits, and data loss prevention techniques are some of the ways that endpoint security helps to safeguard sensitive data while maintaining confidentiality and integrity.

- **Compliance Adherence:** Endpoint security helps companies satisfy regulatory compliance standards like GDPR, HIPAA, and PCI, and DSS.

- **Remote Work Enablement:** As remote work has become more popular, endpoint security helps in reducing the dangers involved by enabling employees to safely access company networks and data from any location.

- **Improved Productivity:** Endpoint security increases efficiency by keeping endpoints and systems safe and operational while limiting the effects of security incidents and decreasing downtime brought on by malware infections or system breaches.

## 6.4 Common features of endpoint security solutions

- **Antivirus and Anti-Malware:** These features help to detect and remove malicious software, viruses, and other threats from endpoints. They help provide real time scanning and signature-based detection.

- **Firewall and Network Filtering:** The traffic that enters and leaves the network is managed by endpoint firewalls. Malicious communication is stopped and unauthorized access is blocked.

- **Device Control:** In order to stop malware from infecting devices and leaking data, device control limits the use of external devices (such as USB drives and external hard drives). It guarantees that devices that are permitted can only connect to endpoints.

- **Application Whitelisting and Blacklisting:** only authorized applications are able to operate on endpoints thanks to whitelisting. Apps that are known to be malicious are blocked by blacklisting.

- **Behavioral Analysis and Heuristics:** These functions keep an eye out for questionable activity on endpoint behavior. They identify anomalies and zero-day risks.

- **Data Loss Prevention (DLP):** Secure data is kept inside endpoints by DLP. Helps for uploads to the cloud and email attachments are among the data flows that it tracks and manages.

- **Patch Management:** This ensures that endpoints have the latest security patches and updates. It helps to reduce vulnerabilities due to outdated software.

- **Encryption:** Helps to encrypt data on endpoints to protect it from unauthorized access. Full-disk encryption secures the entire storage drive.

- **Endpoint Detection and Response (EDR):** Real-time threat detection, investigation, and action are provided by EDR solutions. They gather telemetry information and examine endpoint operations.

- **Multi-Factor Authentication (MFA):** it multiplies the authentication process by demanding a password, token, and biometric. Even in the event that login credentials are hacked, it prevents unwanted access.

## 6.5 Supply Chain Security

Businesses are realizing how important it is to protect their supply chains from hackers by avoiding using unaffiliated providers as entry points. Attacks on supply chains, like the one that happened with SolarWinds, emphasize the necessity of improving supplier and vendor screening and oversight.

**What Is Supply Chain Security?**

When goods, services, and data are transferred across a supply chain, supply chain security refers to protecting their availability, integrity, and confidentiality. Risk mitigation, quality control, and the delivery of goods and services are only a few of the many facets it covers. Other aspects include physical and cyber hazards. Here are some notable key points to understand:

**The Importance of Supply Chain Security**

- **Protecting Confidentiality:** Supply chain security guards against theft and espionage by ensuring that private information, including trade secrets, intellectual property, and customer data, is kept hidden throughout the supply chain.

- **Mitigating Counterfeit Risks:** Businesses may lower the likelihood of fake goods entering their supply networks, which can harm their reputation as a brand

and put customers' health and safety at risk, by putting strong supply chain security measures in place.

- **Ensuring Continuity of Operations:** Through the smooth movement of goods and services even in difficult situations, supply chain security measures help in guaranteeing company continuity by the prevention of disruptions brought on by cyberattacks, natural disasters, or geopolitical events.

- **Compliance with Regulations:** if there is compliance with supply chain security guidelines and standards, it not only keeps businesses out of trouble with the law but also shows stakeholders that they value moral business conduct, which builds credibility.

- **Minimizing Financial Losses:** top organizations can minimize financial losses and preserve shareholder value by proactively addressing supply chain security concerns, which in turn can prevent costly disruptions, theft, or asset destruction.

**Cybersecurity Aspects of Supply Chain Security**

- **Data Protection:** this helps to ensure the privacy and security of data that is being exchanged within the supply chain.

- **System Integrity:** this helps in preventing unauthorized access or tampering with systems and processes.

- **Risk Mitigation:** this helps to Identify and address vulnerabilities that could be exploited across the supply chain.

**Challenges in Supply Chain Security**

- **Legacy Tech:** if there are already existing systems it may not readily support modern security practices.

- **Complex Infrastructure:** Organizations most of the time deal with a mix of cloud, on-premises, and third-party systems.

- **Cost and Effort:** if you want to implement robust security, it requires huge investment in resources and expertise which might not be readily available.

## Strategies for Supply Chain Security

- **Inventory Management:** it's very important to maintain an accurate list of suppliers and vendors.

- **Risk Assessment:** this helps to evaluate cyber risk levels and potential threats.

- **Multi-Tier Approach:** you should consider risks beyond immediate business partners (third, fourth, and subsequent parties).

- **Continuous Monitoring:** this helps to detect anomalous behavior and it will respond promptly.

## 6.6 How to assess the security posture of your supply chain partners

In order to guarantee the availability, confidentiality, and integrity of goods, services, and data, you must evaluate the security posture of your supply chain partners. The following actions are what you should do:

- **Inventory and Classification:** There is a need to maintain an accurate inventory of all your suppliers and vendors. These inventories could be classified based on criticality and the sensitivity of the data they handle.

- **Risk Assessment:** This enables the assessment of the current cyber risk levels associated with each of the partners. Also helps to identify potential vulnerabilities and threats specific to their operations.

- **Frameworks and Tools:** Leverage established frameworks to evaluate security posture and come up with solutions in case of threats:

- **NIST Secure Software Development Framework (SSDF):** Always Considering the entire software development lifecycle and incident response plans.

- **Cybersecurity Assessment Framework (CAF):** this helps in assessing security posture and also mitigate supply chain threats.

- **Supply Chain Levels for Software Artifacts (SLSA):** by prioritizing and incremental implementation of changes. You can use tools that provide insights into security levels, such as Software Delivery Shield.

**VI. Collaboration and Communication:** You can engage in open dialogue with your partners about security practices. Always encourage them to adopt the best practices and improve their security posture.

**VII. Biometric Authentication:** Biometric authentication techniques, like voice recognition, facial recognition, and fingerprint scanning, are gradually taking the place of traditional password-based authentication techniques. These techniques provide customers with increased convenience and enhanced security.

**VIII. Regulatory Compliance:** Organizations are under more pressure than ever to maintain compliance with data protection and privacy laws, thanks to the adoption of rules like the GDPR, CCPA, and, more recently, the California Privacy Rights Act (CPRA). Significant financial fines and harm to one's reputation may arise from noncompliance.

### 6.7 Cybersecurity Skills Gap

There is a growing skills gap as a result of the ongoing shortage of cybersecurity experts. To close this skill gap, businesses are teaming with universities and cybersecurity training providers, investing in and upskilling their current staff. The cybersecurity skills gap is a pressing challenge faced by organizations worldwide. Let us look into this issue deeply and explore potential solutions:

**Understanding the Cybersecurity Skills Gap**

**Magnitude of the Gap:** The need for qualified cybersecurity specialists outweighs the supply of talent by a wide margin. The global cybersecurity workforce deficit has grown by 26.2% from 2021 to 2022, according to the (ISC)2 2022. Cybersecurity Workforce Study, with 3.4 million more people required to successfully secure assets. Because of the ongoing evolution of cyber threats, enterprises are at serious danger to also suffer from this lack.

**Impact on Organizations:**

- **Operational Risks**: because of insufficient cybersecurity expertise it could lead to vulnerabilities, breaches, and disruptions.

- **Financial Consequences:** when there are data breaches and cyber incidents it definitely results in substantial financial losses.

- **Brand Reputation:** if organizations have weak security posture, it enhances reputational damage which most times affects the business negatively.

**Causes of the Gap:**

- **Rapid Technological Advancements:** technologies that are emerging (for example, AI, cloud, IoT) require specialized skills.

- **Complex Threat Landscape:** Cyber threats are diverse and constantly evolving. So it's important to follow up on current trends of threats so that you will not be taken unawares.

- **Lack of Training and Education:** Formal cybersecurity education programs are not keeping pace. It is very necessary to keep pace so that new trends will not elude you.

## Addressing the Gap: Collaborative Solutions

- **Multi Stakeholder Initiatives:** Governments, academia, industry, and nonprofits must collaborate. This will ensure effective manpower generation at all levels and this will in turn create job opportunities in the cybersecurity sector.

- **Investment in Education:** there is a need to promote cybersecurity education at all levels. This will help in sustenance of professionals in the field of cybersecurity

- **Reskilling and Upskilling:** it is very important to encourage professionals from diverse backgrounds to enter the field. When this happens it increases manpower and it will reduce shortages of workforce.

- **Continuous Learning Culture:** it will be very helpful if organizations can foster a culture of continuous learning. This will help improve professionals who are already practicing about new trends in cybersecurity to learn and unlearn.

- **Mentorship Programs:** there will be less gaps if experienced professionals can guide newcomers. This will give rise to orderliness in the field of cybersecurity.

## 6.8 Artificial Intelligence and Machine Learning in Security

Machine learning (ML) and artificial intelligence (AI) are very important to security because they use sophisticated algorithms and data analysis methods to find and eliminate possible risks. Massive volumes of data from many sources, including system logs, network traffic, and user behavior, can be analyzed by AI and ML algorithms to find anomalies or suspicious activity that might point to a security exposure. By constantly adjusting to changing threats and learning from past data, these algorithms help in the improvement of the precision of threat identification. Artificial intelligence (AI)-driven systems are able to recognize anomalies in user behavior by analyzing patterns of activity. These systems are able to identify illegal or hostile activities, such as insider threats or account takeover attacks, by analyzing typical behavior and identifying anomalous actions or access attempts.

In order to identify and categorize various forms of malware, such as viruses, ransomware, and trojans, machine learning algorithms can examine file properties, code patterns, and network activity. These algorithms identify novel variations and zero-day threats by learning from labeled malware samples, allowing for proactive defensive strategies. Fraud detection is achieved by using AI and ML algorithms in industries such as finance and e-commerce. These systems can detect potentially fraudulent activities and flag them for additional investigation by examining transaction patterns, user behavior, and other pertinent data. This helps to prevent financial losses and safeguard user accounts. Software, networks, and infrastructure security flaws can be automatically found by AI-based vulnerability scanners. Organizations are able to efficiently prioritize remediation efforts thanks to these scanners, which simulate attacks, examine system configurations, and rank vulnerabilities according to their potential impact and exploitability.

Platforms for collecting, analyzing, and sharing threat intelligence driven by AI are used to learn about new trends in cyberattacks and threats. These systems can give security teams useful insights to help them proactively defend against new and emerging threats by compiling data from a variety of sources, including as security researchers, forums on the dark web, and open-source feeds. Through the automation of repetitive operations like alarm triage, investigation, and containment, AI-driven security orchestration and automated response (SOAR) solutions can optimize incident response processes. Rapid reaction times and less work for security analysts are made possible by these platforms' integration with current security tools and workflows. Thus organizations' resilience against cyber threats is being enhanced by AI and ML technologies, which are changing the cybersecurity landscape by allowing adaptive defense mechanisms, proactive threat detection, and effective incident response capabilities.

## 6.9 Blockchain Technology for Enhanced Security

Blockchain is a distributed ledger technology that operates on several computers and is decentralized. It is secured and it logs transactions in a transparent, unchangeable, and unhackable manner. To confirm and log transactions, traditional systems depend on a central authority. Hacking, manipulation, or failure could occur at this pivotal point. The single point of failure is eliminated by blockchain, which disperses the transaction data throughout a network of computers (nodes). Every member of the network can see a transaction once it is registered on the blockchain. Because any illegal modifications would be readily noticeable, this transparency lowers the possibility of fraud or manipulation.

The blockchain creates an unchangeable chain of blocks by encrypting each one with the hash of the one before it. A high level of data integrity is ensured by the fact that once a transaction is entered into the blockchain, it is almost permanent and cannot be altered later. Blockchain networks employ consensus techniques, like Proof of Work (PoW) or Proof of Stake (PoS), to verify and reach a consensus over the legitimacy of transactions. If you do this, the possibility of fraudulent or harmful activity is reduced because only valid transactions are uploaded to the blockchain.

With the terms of the agreement directly encoded into the code, smart contracts are self-executing agreements. Without the need for middlemen and a lower chance of mistakes or manipulation, they automatically uphold the terms of the agreement. Transaction data is secured by blockchain using cutting-edge cryptographic algorithms. To sign transactions and confirm their legitimacy, each member of the network is assigned a distinct cryptographic key. Tracking and auditing transactions is made simpler by the transparent and unchangeable nature of blockchain. In sectors where maintaining compliance and traceability is very important for security, such as finance and supply chains, this is especially helpful.

## 6.10 Ethical Considerations in Cybersecurity

This means a variety of values and norms that control how people and organizations behave when protecting digital systems and data are all included in the category of ethical considerations in cybersecurity. Because of the possible effects that cybersecurity practices may have on people, businesses, and society at large, these factors are very important:

- **Privacy:** it is very important to respect an individuals' privacy rights. It is paramount in cybersecurity. This entails collecting only necessary data, securing it from unauthorized access, and being extremely transparent about how data is used and stored.

- **Transparency:** Cybersecurity professionals should be very open and transparent about their actions and the security measures they are implementing. This includes opening up on time about security breaches promptly and accurately, as well as being honest about the limitations of security measures.

- **Integrity:** It is very important to keep systems and data intact. Hackers and security experts shouldn't do anything that jeopardizes data integrity or accuracy, such as faking logs or adjusting security settings.

- **Confidentiality:** Protection of sensitive information from unauthorized access is a fundamental ethical principle. This involves implementing strong encryption, access controls, and other security measures to safeguard data from internal and external threats.

- **Accountability:** IT specialists need to own up to their mistakes and accept accountability for the choices they made. Thus, to prevent future occurrences of the same type of security disaster, it is necessary to first own one's faults, then learn from them.

- **Lawfulness:** The applicable laws, rules, and industry standards should be followed by cybersecurity specialists. In carrying out security testing, this entails abiding by data protection regulations, protecting intellectual property rights, and using ethical hacking practices.

- **Minimizing Harm:** It is important to take steps so as to reduce the possible harm that cybersecurity procedures and security events may cause. This includes putting in place efficient incident response strategies, helping those who are impacted, and lessening the effects of security flaws.

- **Promoting Security Awareness:** In order to promote a culture of security, it is imperative that individuals and organizations get education regarding cybersecurity risks and best practices. This entails educating people on security procedures, encouraging appropriate cyber hygiene practices, and increasing knowledge of frequent risks.

## 6.11 Ethical Hacking and Penetration Testing

Two cybersecurity techniques that are used to find and fix vulnerabilities in computer systems, networks, and applications are penetration testing and ethical hacking.

- **Ethical Hacking:** In order to find gaps in a system's security, authorized professionals, also referred to as "white hat hackers," engage in ethical hacking by simulating cyberattacks. With the system owner's consent, these people employ the same methods and resources as malevolent hackers. Finding security holes early on is the aim, so as to prevent actual attackers from taking advantage of them.

- **Penetration Testing:** Within the field of ethical hacking, penetration testing is also known as pen testing. To determine a system's security posture, it entails launching controlled attacks on it. To estimate the possible impact of an actual cyberattack, pen testers try to take advantage of flaws in the system's applications, infrastructure, and rules. Organizations can easily use this to identify their security strengths and weaknesses and prioritize remedial actions with the aid of this procedure.

Simply put, by detecting and reducing security problems before bad actors can take advantage of them, penetration testing and ethical hacking are essential tools for protecting companies against online threats. In order to safeguard sensitive information and guarantee the availability, integrity, and confidentiality of digital assets, these procedures are very important parts of the cybersecurity plan.

**Responsible Disclosure Policies**

In order to make it easier for people to disclose and fix security flaws in their systems, goods, or services, corporations have created responsible disclosure policies, also referred to as coordinated vulnerability disclosure or responsible vulnerability disclosure. Here is a detailed explanation:

**Purpose:** Encouragement of security researchers, ethical hackers, and other persons to responsibly report vulnerabilities to the organization is the main objective of a responsible disclosure policy. This way, before bad actors take advantage of the situation, the business can quickly resolve the problem and reduce any potential dangers.

**Key Principles:**

- **Transparency**: The policy should specify how vulnerabilities should be reported, along with the best ways to get in touch with each other and the appropriate channels for responsible disclosure.

- **Collaboration**: In order to verify, duplicate, and comprehend the nature and consequences of the vulnerability, organizations pledge to collaborate with the reporting party.

- **Timeliness:** In order to guarantee that vulnerabilities are fixed as soon as possible, all parties commit to timely communication and action throughout the disclosure process.

- **Acknowledgement:** A lot of firms encourage researchers to follow the disclosure process by providing awards or acknowledgment to those who properly reveal vulnerabilities.

**Reporting Process:**

In order to report vulnerabilities, researchers or individuals usually follow the organization's established procedure, which can include using a specialized vulnerability disclosure platform, submitting a form on the organization's website, or getting in touch with a specified email address. Any proof-of-concept code or demos that can help the company comprehend and validate the problem should be included in the report, along with comprehensive details regarding the vulnerability, including its nature, effect, and potential for exploitation.

**Response and Resolution:**

As soon as a vulnerability report is received, the security team of the company or other pertinent parties evaluate it to confirm that the issue is real and serious. The company creates and implements a plan to fix the vulnerability when it has been verified, this may entail creating updates, patches, or workarounds to deal with the problem. In order to give the reporting party updates on progress and fix release schedules, the organization stays in contact with them during the resolution process.

**Publication of Findings:**

A security advisory or disclosure notice may be published by the company to notify users, clients, and the larger security community about the vulnerability and the efforts made to resolve it when the vulnerability has been effectively mitigated. The company and the reporting party may also work together to draft joint advisories or research papers for distribution in security forums or conferences, depending on the seriousness and effect of the vulnerability. In order to properly detect and resolve security vulnerabilities, enterprises and security researchers must work together, and this is made possible by responsible disclosure rules. Organizations may improve their security posture and shield their users and clients from any cyber attacks by putting in place clear policies and procedures for reporting and fixing vulnerabilities.

# Chapter 7

## 7.1 Careers in Cybersecurity

Safeguarding computer networks, systems, and data from unwanted access, malicious attacks, or other harm is the focus of the field of cybersecurity. Protecting digital assets from cyber threats is the goal of cybersecurity. Let us look at some of the common careers in cybersecurity:

**I. Security Analyst:** In order to prevent cyberattacks, security analysts install security measures, look into infractions, and monitor computer networks for security breaches. In order to improve an organization's overall security posture, they examine security data and create strategies to avert threats.

**II. Penetration Tester (Ethical Hacker):** If you want to find weaknesses in networks, applications, and systems, penetration testers imitate cyberattacks. Through the use of vulnerabilities, they evaluate the efficacy of current security protocols and suggest enhancements to reduce potential hazards.

**III. Security Engineer:** Infrastructure protection is provided by security engineers through the design, implementation, and upkeep of security systems. In order to safeguard data confidentiality and integrity and prevent unwanted access, they design firewalls, encryption techniques, and other security-related technologies.

**IV. Security Consultant:** Companies that want to strengthen their security posture might get advice from security consultants. Along with creating security policies and procedures, risk assessments and regulatory compliance advice are also provided by them. Experts in security best practices may also instruct staff members.

**V. Incident Responder:** Data breaches, malware infections, and denial-of-service attacks are examples of security occurrences that incident responders are responsible for managing. In order to contain the damage, they look into the underlying causes of disasters and create plans to stop them from happening in the future.

**VI. Cryptographer:** To ensure safe data transmission and storage, cryptographers specialize in developing and decoding cryptographic algorithms. They are essential to the creation of digital signatures, encryption methods, and other cryptographic techniques that help to safeguard private data.

**VII. Security Architect:** An organization's comprehensive security architecture is created by security architects, who take into account things like business needs, technology capabilities, and regulatory compliance. To help with the application of security measures throughout the organization, they create security frameworks and standards that should be followed.

**VIII. Security Operations Center (SOC) Analyst:** Security event monitoring and analysis is done in real time by SOC analysts to identify and address possible threats. Using security information and event management (SIEM) systems, they look into unusual activity and correlate data from different sources.

## 7.2 Overview of Cybersecurity Roles

Now, let us explore the intriguing field of cybersecurity jobs. Protecting our digital environment from threats and attacks is a vital responsibility of these people. I will provide you a summary of the many kinds of cybersecurity jobs, along with their duties and typical pay.

**The 12 types of cybersecurity roles:**

**Computer Forensic Analyst:**

- **Duties:** They help to assess devices and systems to recover data. They assist law enforcement in criminal investigations related to cybercrime.

- **Average Salary:** Approximately $46,146 per year.

**IT Security Specialist:**

- **Duties:** their main responsibility is to collaborate with teams to develop strategies for protecting devices and systems within an organization. They identify vulnerabilities and strengthen security measures.

- **Average Salary:** Around $57,787 per year.

**Security Manager:**

- **Duties:** Security managers oversee security efforts within an organization. They manage IT teams, develop cybersecurity strategies, and establish rules and regulations.

- **Average Salary:** Approximately $64,000 per year.

**Security Engineer:**

- **Duties:** These guys focuses on implementing critical security measures across an organization. They help to troubleshoot and enhance security protocols.

- **Average Salary:** About $76,009 per year.

**Network Security Administrator:**

- **Duties:** Network security administrators configure and monitor network security tools, firewalls, and intrusion detection systems.

- **Average Salary:** the salary varies based on experience and location.

**Penetration Tester (Ethical Hacker):**

- **Duties:** Penetration testers simulate cyberattacks to identify vulnerabilities in systems. They help organizations strengthen their defenses.

- **Average Salary:** from $80,000 to $120,000 per year.

**Security Consultant:**

- **Duties:** Security consultants help to assess an organization's security posture, recommend improvements, and develop risk mitigation strategies.

- **Average Salary:** Varies based on expertise and project scope.

**Incident Response Analyst:**

- **Duties:** These analysts investigate and respond to security incidents, including data breaches and cyberattacks.

- **Average Salary:** Around $70,000 to $90,000 per year.

## Security Architect:

- **Duties:** Security architects design and build secure systems, considering both technical and business requirements.

- **Average Salary:** Typically $100,000 or more per year.

## Cryptographer:

- **Duties:** Cryptographers create and analyze cryptographic algorithms to protect data and communications.

- **Average Salary:** Varies based on specialization and experience.

**Security Auditor:**

- **Duties:** Security auditors assess an organization's security controls, policies, and compliance with regulations.

- **Average Salary:** Approximately $70,000 to $100,000 per year.

**Malware Analyst:**

- **Duties:** Malware analysts study malicious software to understand its behavior and develop countermeasures.

- **Average Salary:** Varies based on expertise and industry

## 7.3 Education and Certification Paths

Together, we will look into the fascinating realm of cybersecurity credentials and courses. There are several avenues you can pursue if you want to grow in your profession or if you are just getting started:

**1. Education Paths:**

**a. Associate Degrees:** An associate degree prepares students for entry-level roles in cybersecurity. It provides foundational knowledge and practical skills. You should consider pursuing an associate degree if you're new to the field and want a solid starting point.

**b. Bachelor's Degrees:** Bachelor's degrees in cybersecurity are available both online and in-person. They offer comprehensive training and cover various aspects of security. A bachelor's degree is ideal if you're aiming for mid-level positions and want a deeper understanding of cybersecurity concepts.

**c. Master's Degrees:** In order to further specialize, universities offer master's degrees in cybersecurity. Advanced subjects and research are covered in these programs. If you want to work in cutting-edge research or want to climb the leadership ladder, get a master's degree.

**d. Doctoral Degrees:** Doctorate degrees in cybersecurity are offered for individuals desiring the greatest level of proficiency. These courses emphasize creativity and investigation., and academia.

## 2. Certification Paths:

Certificates confirm your knowledge and improve your employability, but formal education is still necessary. Some well-liked cybersecurity certificates are as follows:

**Certified Information Systems Security Professional (CISSP):**

- **Description:** CISSP is a sought-after credential that demonstrates expertise in designing, implementing, and monitoring cybersecurity programs.

- **Target Roles:** Chief Information Security Officer (CISO), security consultant, and more.

- **Average Salary:** Up to $193,081.

**Certified Information Systems Auditor (CISA):**

- **Description:** CISA focuses on auditing, assessing, and managing information systems.

- **Target Roles:** IT auditor, compliance analyst, and more.

**CompTIA Security+:**

- **Description:** Entry-level certification covering foundational security concepts.

- **Target Roles:** Security analyst, network administrator, and more.

**Certified Ethical Hacker (CEH):**

- **Description:** CEH certified ethical hacking skills, emphasizing vulnerability assessment and penetration testing.

- **Target Roles:** Penetration tester, security engineer, and more.

**Certified Information Security Manager (CISM):**

- **Description:** CISM focuses on information risk management and governance.

- **Target Roles:** Security manager, risk analyst, and more.

**Offensive Security Certified Professional (OSCP):**

- **Description:** OSCP validates practical skills in penetration testing.

- **Target Roles:** Penetration tester, security consultant, and more.

Having certifications gives you a competitive edge and enhances your educational background. Based on your hobbies and job objectives, make sure you choose your certificates to suit all that you want to do. Happy learning

## 7.4 Conclusion

The stronghold of cybersecurity serves as our steadfast protector in this digital world of today, when every click may result in a possible cyberattack. It heroically protects our virtual worlds from malicious hackers and sneaky spyware, much like a contemporary superhero. But as we make our way through this constantly changing environment, one thing becomes quite evident: cybersecurity isn't an option, it's a must. Imagine living in a world where cybersecurity does not exist. As hackers walk freely through our digital corridors, stealing confidential data, upsetting vital infrastructure, and causing mayhem without repercussions, chaos reigns supreme. It's a dystopian nightmare akin to a Hollywood film, but without the comforting confidence that the heroes will ultimately triumph.

Fortunately, things aren't nearly as bad as they seem. We are equipped with the know-how and resources necessary to defeat these online enemies thanks to cybersecurity. Our powerful armory to safeguard our data and maintain our digital lifestyle includes firewalls, encryption, multi-factor authentication, and penetration testing. Don't fool yourself, though; the fight is far from over. Cybercriminals' techniques are evolving along with technology. Their persistent search for flaws to exploit and openings to breach keeps them hidden in the shadows. There's an ongoing struggle for supremacy between the two sides in this game of cat and mouse.

However, there is optimism in sight despite the odds that might be against us. Every new cyberthreat presents an opportunity for creativity and adaptation. We strengthen our defenses, grow from our mistakes, and overcome our past. It's evidence of the tenacity of the human spirit and the inventiveness of our species.

Therefore, let us continue to fight for cybersecurity in all of its manifestations and be ever-vigilant in the face of possible attacks. Because in this digital age, maintaining security is essential to survival rather than merely convenience. And we can make sure that our digital future is both bright and safe if we have the correct attitude and resources at our disposal.

## 7.5 Appendix

**Glossary of terms**

**1. Malware**: this refers to any software designed to cause damage to a computer, server, client, or computer network.

**2. Phishing:** A cyber attack where the attacker disguises as a trustworthy entity in electronic communication to trick individuals into revealing sensitive information.

**3. Firewall:** This is a network security system that monitors and controls incoming and outgoing network traffic based on predetermined security rules.

**4. Encryption:** This means the process of converting information or data into a code to prevent unauthorized access.

**5. Vulnerability:** A weakness in a system's security that could be exploited by a threat actor.

**6. DDoS (Distributed Denial of Service):** a cyberattack when the attacker tries to overwhelm the target with a torrent of internet traffic in order to render a computer or network resource unavailable to its intended users.

**7. Zero-day Exploit**: A cyber attack that occurs on the same day a vulnerability is discovered, before a fix or patch is available from its creator.

**8. Two-factor Authentication (2FA):** A security process in which the user provides two different authentication factors to verify themselves.

**9. Patch**: A piece of software designed to update a computer program or its supporting data, to fix or improve it.

**10. Penetration Testing (Pen Testing):** A simulated cyber attack against a computer system to check for exploitable vulnerabilities.

**11. Social Engineering:** A tactic that is commonly used by cyber criminals that relies on human interaction to manipulate individuals into giving out confidential information.

**12. Data Breach**: An incident where sensitive, protected, or confidential data is accessed or disclosed without authorization.

**13. Endpoint Security:** The practice of securing end-user devices such as desktops, laptops, and mobile devices from cyber threats.

**14. Cyber Threat Intelligence (CTI):** Information that is collected, processed, and analyzed to understand cyber threats and vulnerabilities.

**15. Ransomware:** A type of malware that encrypts a victim's files and demands payment, usually in cryptocurrency, to decrypt them.

**16. Intrusion Detection System (IDS):** A security tool designed to monitor network or system activities for malicious activities or policy violations.

**17. Antivirus Software:** this is a oftware that is designed to detect, prevent, and remove malware from a computer system.

**18. Cybersecurity Incident Response:** The process of managing the impact of cybersecurity incidents, including identifying, investigating, and resolving them.

**19. Cybersecurity Framework**: This is a set of guidelines or rules, best practices, and standards designed to help organizations manage and improve their cybersecurity posture.

**20. Data Loss Prevention (DLP):** A strategy for preventing the unauthorized transmission of sensitive information outside of an organization's network.

**21. Secure Socket Layer (SSL) / Transport Layer Security (TLS):** these are protocols that provide secure communication over a computer network by encrypting data sent between a client and server.

**22. Access Control:** This is the process of limiting access to resources or information only to authorized users or systems.

**23. Network Segmentation**: This entails the practice of dividing a computer network into smaller subnetworks to improve security and performance.

**24. Incident Response Plan (IRP):** this is a documented, structured approach for responding to and managing cybersecurity incidents.

**25. Cybersecurity Awareness Training**: this is an education and training programs designed to educate employees and individuals about cybersecurity risks, best practices, and procedures.

**26. Multi-factor Authentication (MFA):** this is an authentication method that requires the user to provide two or more verification factors to gain access.

**27. Blockchain:** This can be described as decentralized, distributed ledger technology used to record transactions across multiple computers in a secure and transparent manner.

**28. Cybersecurity Risk Assessment:** This is the process of identifying, analyzing, and evaluating potential cybersecurity risks to an organization's assets, systems, and data.

**29. Social Engineering Toolkit (SET):** This is a framework that is used for simulating social engineering attacks and testing the security awareness of individuals and organizations.

**30. Virtual Private Network (VPN):** this is a technology that creates a secure, encrypted connection over a less secure network, such as the internet, to ensure privacy and security.

**31. Honeypot:** this can be described as a decoy system or resource that is set up to attract and deceive attackers, allowing security professionals to monitor and analyze their behavior.

**32. Rootkit:** This is a type of malicious software that enables unauthorized access to a computer or network while hiding its presence from users and security tools.

**33. Cyber Threat Hunting:** this is a proactive and iterative process of searching for threats within an organization's networks and systems, often using advanced analytics and forensic tools.

**34. Security Information and Event Management (SIEM):** this is a software solution that provides real-time analysis of security alerts generated by network hardware and applications.

**35. Cybersecurity Governance:** This is a framework and processes established to ensure that cybersecurity risks are managed appropriately at all levels of an organization.

**36. Secure Development Lifecycle (SDLC):** This is a set of practices and processes used to design, develop, and deploy software securely, with a focus on identifying and addressing security vulnerabilities early in the development process.

**37. Cybersecurity Operations Center (CSOC):** This is a centralized facility responsible for continuously monitoring and managing an organization's security posture, detecting and responding to security incidents, and coordinating incident response efforts.

**38. Firmware**: this is a software that is embedded into hardware devices to control their operation, often requiring security updates to address vulnerabilities.

**39. Threat Intelligence Sharing:** This is the practice of sharing information about cybersecurity threats, vulnerabilities, and attacks among organizations, industries, and government agencies to improve collective defenses.

**40. Red Team / Blue Team:** Two teams within an organization that simulate attacks (Red Team) and defend against them (Blue Team) to test and improve cybersecurity defenses and incident response capabilities.

**41. Data Encryption Standard (DES):** this is a symmetric-key algorithm that is used for encrypting and decrypting data, although it's considered outdated due to its susceptibility to brute-force attacks.

**42. Cyber Insurance:** this is an insurance coverage designed to protect organizations from financial losses resulting from cyber attacks, data breaches, and other cyber incidents.

**43. Security Operations Center (SOC):** This can be described as a centralized team responsible for monitoring, detecting, analyzing, and responding to cybersecurity incidents and threats.

**44. Internet of Things (IoT) Security:** These are practices and measures implemented to secure connected devices and networks in the Internet of Things ecosystem, including smart devices, wearables, and industrial sensors.

**45. Cyber Kill Chain:** this can be defined as a framework used to describe the stages of a cyber attack, from reconnaissance to exfiltration, helping organizations understand and defend against advanced threats.

Happy learning with this book my friend, God bless you!!!

www.ingramcontent.com/pod-product-compliance
Lightning Source LLC
Chambersburg PA
CBHW052146220526
45471CB00004B/1552